This Bookish Inclination

From a child I was fond of Reading
and all the little money that came into my
Hands was ever laid out in Books...
This Bookish Inclination at length determined
my Father to make me a Printer.

BENJAMIN FRANKLIN

Founder of the first public library
in the United States

Designed by Felicity Frisbie

Photos: Arlington Heights Historical Society
unless otherwise specified

Printed in the United States of America
by BookCrafters, Inc., Chelsea, Michigan

Typography by Chief City Graphics, Pontiac, Illinois

ISBN 0-9617830-0-1

This Bookish Inclination

The Story Of
The Arlington Heights Memorial Library
1887–1987

BY MARGERY FRISBIE

ILLUSTRATIONS BY FELICITY FRISBIE

Friends Of The Arlington Heights Memorial Library
Arlington Heights, Illinois
1987

Contents

Foreword

Who would have thought the history of a library would be exciting? No epiphanies. No Armageddons. But it *is* exciting. Ideas in books have moved the world: The Bible, *Common Sense, Das Kapital, Uncle Tom's Cabin.*

Ideas can slay the dragons of ignorance, prejudice, and tyranny. The library—this library—is yet another fortress, a bastion, a strong point, in the line of defenses against the dark forces of barbarism.

So the people who built all this, carefully, over the years, like an intellectual cathedral, stone by stone, book by book, deserve to be remembered. It is fitting to celebrate them, although their deeds speak for themselves on the shelves and in the eager hands of readers, young and old. They provided the weapons. The battle goes on. It will be won.

Frank J. Dempsey
Executive Librarian
Arlington Heights Memorial Library
November, 1986

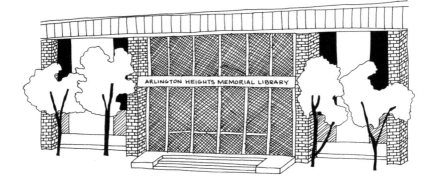

Introduction

When veteran library board member Richard Frisbie was running for his fourth term in 1981, he assumed that any of the scores of patrons who climbed the library steps any Saturday morning would be a likely signer for the petition necessary to get his name on the ballot. Having been quoted on library matters in the local paper for years, he expected some name recognition. He also took it for granted that any frequent patron knew there was a library board, an elected body of citizens who made major policy decisions. He was wrong. Not only had no Saturday morning patron heard of Frisbie, almost no one had heard of a library board, knew how it functioned, why it was necessary, how it served them. Once Frisbie explained, people signed his petition. Some may even have felt a surprised gratitude for his long years of serving them.

I know I came to feel a surprised gratitude as I learned the story of how this great library came to be. Like Kay Anderson whose account begins the book, I probably made the Arlington Heights Memorial Library my first stop when I moved to town. Only when I began to write this book, however, did I begin to credit the library board members and staff responsible for a third of a century of enlightenment, entertainment, and gratification. For the joy of becoming deeply acquainted with this library, the Village of Arlington Heights and its people, I thank assistant head of youth services Pat Craig, whose faith and enthusiasm undergirded every step of this project; executive librarian Frank J. Dempsey, for his valuable support; and the Friends of the Arlington Heights Memorial Library, who generously underwrote this enterprise—another of their many gifts to the villagers.

The book would have been five more years in the making without the careful culling of sources for pertinent fact, incident, and description by reference librarian Kathrine Shackley and her volunteer assistants, Theresa Blackberg and Frances Boyd, who put in "endless hours." There would be no book at all, of course, but for the testimony of all the witnesses to the library's creation who patiently answered my questions into a tape recorder and created in my head this picture of the Arlington Heights Memorial Library—its first one hundred years.

Margery Frisbie
October 15, 1986
Arlington Heights, Illinois

8

1.
A Warm Reception

A young family moved from Chicago's Austin neighborhood to Arlington Heights in the early fifties, one of the many that swelled the population from 8,768 to 64,584 in twenty years. Once they were settled in their Georgian home in the Scarsdale subdivision, they began to scout out their new town, starting with the library.

Neighbors pointed out the location on the second floor of the village hall, at the point made by Davis and Wing Streets. Mother and children climbed the intimidatingly long flight of stairs into an ample, handsome room divided by orange crates into sections for the children and the adults.

"The sun was shining in the Romanesque windows," Kay Anderson reports years later, "the room was pleasant. What struck us most, though, was the warmth of our reception.

"We had frequented a lot of libraries. We'd been cautioned to be quiet and we'd been rebuked when we weren't quiet enough. We'd often had the feeling that the librarians grudged us the books as they checked them out.

"But that afternoon in Arlington Heights we were made to feel as if we were welcome in the library, and as if we were welcome to the books. That was one of our earliest experiences in town, and a significant one. It made us glad we had moved here."

Peggy Anderson, who took her first books out of the Arlington Heights Public Library that afternoon, was one day to return the favor. Author of *Nurse,* which was subsequently

9

made into a television series, and *Children's Hospital,* she has now, in a sense, put books back into the library she once took them out of.

The hospitality the Andersons experienced that afternoon had been part of the library character since the Misses Shepard opened the living room of their faded frame house at 310 North Dunton Avenue to Arlington Heights readers in 1894. "The Shepards loved company. They adored it when people dropped in," an octogenarian recalls today, thinking back to her first experience as a book borrower. "Miss Effie would sit down beside me and read me a little bit of a story she admired, enough to get me interested. I wouldn't be able to wait to get home so I could read the rest of it."

As the library graduated from the Shepards' living room to the hall at North School, to the Peoples Bank building, to the village hall and, finally, to its own quarters on Belmont and

Shepard House, library site, 1894-1909

then Dunton Avenue, that same spirit was preserved. The staff consciously tried to forestall any inclination toward possessiveness. Perhaps librarian Mary Lee Ewalt expressed it best when she told the architect for the Dunton Avenue building that, given her druthers, she'd have the stacks on the outside of the building all the way round the block and never badger anyone to return a book until he or she was ready.

The stacks are not ranged along the exterior walls. That never became a reality. But the impulse that shaped that aspiration is a reality. Patrons today mark the effects of that sustained policy.

The library's generous character was formed by Effie and Lucy Shepard, Mary Lee Ewalt, and a host of other citizens and staff members who created the great welcomes and the distinguished collection.

Youngsters looking up at the handsome, drop-shot limestone building that stretches over a city block and a half may be impressed with the size of the library relevant to the size of the village. They don't question how it came to be. They don't wonder who bought the first book, who stamped it out, who read it. They accept the library as they would Mount Everest. It is "there." Villages just have libraries.

If they were to investigate its origins they would discover that just as the hospitality which is the library's benchmark was created by the staff that checked out the books over the years, so each aspect of the library was formed by the character of cooperating villagers who believed in books as "great helpers in the civilization of men," as an early library promoter wrote.

Those villagers were as generous with their time and energy as the library itself was with the books. Florence Hendrickson, board president during the move from Belmont Avenue to Dunton Avenue, always cautioned prospective

11

board members that serving was a full-time job. That prescription was not out of line with actual practice. There were board members so active that their associates wondered how they managed to perform the tasks necessary to support their families.

The results speak for the system. There would be a library in Arlington Heights in any case, but not the library there is if it were not for the board members who "worked full time at it," the ladies in the Reading Circle who dreamed it in 1887, the Arlington Heights Woman's Club who tended it at North School, the Tri-Sigma group at the Methodist Church who prodded the community into approving a library tax in 1926, staff members who believed in the work they were doing, and librarians who meant that the books should be openhandedly available to the townspeople.

Hundreds of people come through the doors of the Arlington Heights Memorial Library on Dunton Avenue every week of the year to attend concerts, movies, meetings, craft shows, flower-arranging classes, and to borrow one million items a year—seventy-five percent of them books.

They come from both ends of the village, from the tollway on the south and the Lake County border on the north, to what is almost the exact geographical center of the village.

Not only is the library geographically central, it is also on historic ground. The library's footings dig into what was a quarter section claimed by Arlington Heights' founding family. Asa Dunton, a stonecutter from Oswego, New York, filed his claim for 160 acres for himself, and 160 acres for each of his two sons, in 1836. After they received full title to the land in 1841, the family moved to Lemont, Illinois, where they could return to stonecutting, their trade.

William, one of the sons, was the first to come back. Initially, he farmed. But when he saw a chance to persuade the

12

William Dunton

Illinois and Wisconsin Railroad to lay its track through his farm, he subdivided his land which included the present site of the library.

Historically, geographically rooted, the library is also culturally a reflection of the people who have settled Arlington Heights. When artists intend to show their subjects as persons of scholarship and learning, they invariably depict them, as Botticelli did St. Augustine, in book-lined studies, poring over heavy volumes.

In that sense, the Arlington Heights Memorial Library is a self-portrait of the people of the village. They have created this great institution, have given "to airy nothing a local habitation and a name," as Theseus cries in *A Midsummer Night's Dream.*

The library was an airy nothing when six women dreamed of it in 1887. One hundred years later that dream has a local habitation, "a book-lined study" where villagers show themselves as persons of scholarship and learning as they gather in the great library the people of Arlington Heights have created.

2.
Book Friends

Life on the Illinois prairie was primitive and lonely when Almeda Wood married the founder of Arlington Heights in her family's twelve by fourteen foot cabin in 1845. But William Dunton, who took her to live in a dressed-lumber house on the high ground where the Chicago and North Western tracks would one day cross Arlington Heights Road, was immensely resourceful.

Almeda recounted for years how he bent two saplings and attached them to a dry goods box to make a sleigh, a "jumper," to carry the two of them to visit Almeda's new in-laws southwest of Chicago that first winter.

Later, William was quick to see that his claim's chance for fortune depended on the railway that Chicagoans were projecting out along Rand Road. He speculated that a wide

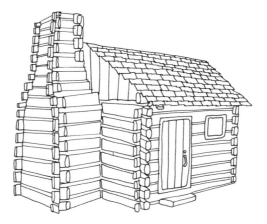

gauge track cutting through his property could turn his quarter section into a commercial bonanza.

Bonanza might be a little thick for a collection of frame houses awash in a sea of sloughs. But the New Englanders and New Yorkers who had farmed the good out of their rocky plots back east were impressed with the rich loam of Illinois and the opportunities it provided, just as Louis Joliet had been one hundred and eighty years before when he noted that there was "no better soil either for corn, for vines, for any other fruit whatever."

The Easterners had suffered interminable train rides behind engines that spewed sparks and, sometimes, prairie fires; mal de mer on lake boats; boredom on canal barges, and bumps in covered wagons to come west. They meant to yoke the prairie soil that burgeoned with stunning wildflowers and grass as tall as a man on horseback.

A few years later, those first settlers from the East copied William Dunton's enterprise and sold their farms to a second swell of immigrants, Germans fleeing failed revolution, taxes, and conscription.

The Yankees moved off the farms into William Dunton's town along the railroad tracks. The Germans settled behind the plows, making a much better job of farming than the earlier settlers had done. Back home the Germans had

15

learned that they couldn't farm their land down to a nubbin. They had discovered how to rotate their crops, how to fertilize effectively. These lessons were not lost on the good Illinois earth.

The Yankee women who now had frame houses on mud streets within walking distance of the train to Chicago had brought west with them a certain mercantile cunning common to Yankees and a hunger for intellectual stimulation that New England had bred in their minds.

Sleepy Hollow was part of their history and Rip Van Winkle an old friend. They'd heard about Margaret Fuller's "conversations," even if they had never attended one. They'd learned part of their history from *Evangeline* and *The Courtship of Miles Standish.*

If they could not yet quote Emerson and Longfellow, then an educational movement coming out of their remembered East was fast catching up on them to remedy that lack.

The Chautauqua Movement was a response to the craving of hundreds of thousands of people across the country, in the Middle West particularly, for knowledge. "To know, only to know, is the earnest cry of multitudes of our fellows," the Chautauqua registrar said of this constituency.

By bringing lecturers and artists to rural communities and by offering correspondence courses which opened up history and literature and art and science to those starved for culture, the Chautauqua phenomenon gave hope and dignity to the frustrated ambitions of thousands. Theodore Roosevelt is said to have called Chautauqua "the most American thing in America." Others suggested that with the exception, possibly, of the Model T, no other American institution left a greater impact on the social and cultural life of the country people of the United States.

Between 1878 and 1898, a quarter of a million people who

hadn't been able to go to college, and some who had, studied Chautauqua in ten thousand circles. They pored over texts during the week and gathered every seven days to have "classroom recitation," combining a pleasant social occasion with a broadening of the mind.

Chautauqua came to Arlington Heights with a new school principal and his wife who had participated in study groups in the small central Illinois town from which they had come.

The winter of 1886-1887 was as harsh as some of the discipline in the town's religious schools. Hugging her wood-stove that boldly frigid season, the principal's wife made up her mind that she would thaw out her neighbors' shivering bodies with the fire of learning, just as effectively as those flatirons wrapped in blankets which toasted their toes in bed. She would start a Chautauqua circle in her home.

Five of her friends were invited to Mrs. Amos Walker's home at the corner of Evergreen and Eastman, just east of the First Methodist Church, a two-story frame building at Dunton and St. James. Two of the five women were daughter and daughter-in-law of the Reverend Thomas Goodfellow who had been pastor of the church and died in a fatal accident. One was a teacher in the Chicago school system, another a graduate of Wheaton College, and the fifth, evidently without that sort of credential, had a "superior intellect."

Actually, they all had that. They were superior women in an era when women were discouraged from seeking higher education. Like Elizabeth Walker, they had roots in New England cultivation, and they wanted wings. They liked Mrs. Walker's notion to emulate Chautauqua. They agreed to meet every week to do it.

They decided to call their group The Reading Circle and chose Elizabeth Walker as their leader. They were ready to welcome other women who, like them, wanted to reach past prairie town life to the greater world beyond.

To initiate their ambitious grasp at world history and literature the women read Benjamin Franklin's account of how he parlayed good pronunciation (a concern of the women), a good grasp of history and literature (their aim), and acquaintance with the trade of governance into a career that served him and his country well. "I was the youngest son," Franklin wrote, "and the youngest child but two, and was born in Boston, New England."

The women read and were launched on an enterprise which culminated in the Arlington Heights Memorial Library in the next century. They could not have realized how appropriate the choice of Franklin's autobiography was: they inaugurated the library in Arlington Heights by reading the life of the founder of U.S. public libraries. For Benjamin Franklin established the first lending library in the country in Philadelphia in 1731.

Like the women in The Reading Circle, Franklin was "fond of reading, and all the little money that came into my hands was ever laid out in books."

It was Franklin's "bookish inclination" that determined his father to make him a printer. The women's bookish inclination led another way, the collecting instead of the making of books.

Not content with the knowledge they were gathering, the women were eager to articulate correctly. Each of them set out to improve her pronunciation. To achieve the hoped-for purity of diction, each carried a small pronouncing manual, thought to be the best available, compiled from such authorities as Webster, Walker, and Worcester.

Serious about this nicety, the women delegated a member at each meeting to take up a listening post at the back so that she could report all pronunciation lapses at refreshment time. Sometimes the women added a general test on pronunciation to the agenda.

No one seemed to be offended by this emphasis on enunciating the "g" in "ing" endings or articulating the diphthongs neatly, because the group began to grow at once. In two years there were eighteen women meeting weekly in their homes. The critic continued to report at the close of those meetings until 1897.

From the very start the women began to stockpile books against the day when they would establish a public library. That was part of their Arlington Heights plan from the outset. They were not content to work only at their personal intellectual development. They wanted what Helen Keller called the "sweet gracious discourse of book friends" for their neighbors and their neighbors' children.

Self-improvement and village improvement advanced hand in hand, and book by book. By 1894 the diligent women in The Reading Circle had garnered enough books at Olive Dietrich's home to open a Lilliputian library.

Two friendly maiden ladies who thought they would enjoy the stimulation of books and readers offered to open the living room in their one-and-a-half-story frame house at 310 North Dunton two afternoons a week to club members and their families. Before long, the little library was open to the whole village, to all those who wished to pursue the agreeable custom of reading by lamplight when their chores were done.

Lucy Shepard, chunky and cheerful, her bun of black hair caught up in a net, was the librarian until she accepted the post of teacher at Wilson School on Palatine Road. When Lucy began leaving the weathered frame house just north of the Presbyterian Church manse for the trek along wooden sidewalks and mud roads to oversee her country school, Effie took up the duties of readying the books for borrowers. She

19

held steady at that helm until 1909.

The Shepards' little house was built by Peter Bradley for whom Arlington Heights was named for a short time—as long as it took to discover another town called Bradley out near Kankakee. It faced east so the "library" room wasn't especially sunny on Tuesday and Friday afternoons when the patrons, mostly children, arrived, even though Effie Shepard kept the shades up. But, like her sister, Effie Shepard brought warmth to the room with her friendly, pleasant manner. A tall gaunt woman, Effie Shepard made an effort to match the child with the book, often telling bits of the narrative to get the youngster interested.

Children from all over the village marked their library days twice a week and trundled down the wooden sidewalks with the gaps every few feet to catch unwitting heels, up to the Shepards' front door. Like *The Little Lame Prince* in Miss Mulock's popular fantasy, which they could find on the shelves, the children soared past the modest limits of their Midwest village as they read Hawthorne's *Wonder Book* or Robert Louis Stevenson's *Treasure Island* by the kerosene lamp at the kitchen table after supper—just as the women in The Reading Circle had planned.

Often their parents went along to the library for the collection of adults' books kept pace with the children's during the Shepard years. Even after the circle regrouped as the Arlington Heights Woman's Club in 1896, the women continued their strenuous self-education. At a typical meeting that year Elinore Haynes read a paper on the works of Sir Walter Scott, Hattie Farwell (grand-daughter of Asa Dunton) one on Edward IV, and Emily Draper one on the life of Louis XI. All the members contributed quotations from Scott at the roll call.

By 1900 there were fifty members in the woman's club,

largely because a woman's existence was becoming less arduous. Many of them no longer had to help with the morning and evening milking. They could now buy lovely lengths of cloth from the Marshall Field's wholesale division at Mr. Redeker's store at Vail and Campbell. They could put their minds to work for themselves, and their energies to work for the village.

Doggedly, they tackled Green's history of the English people and fleshed out the historical skeleton with forays into English literature. But not everyone was in favor of such hard work. One timid soul suggested they should read the Mary J. Holmes novels instead.

She was overruled by readers who preferred Sir Walter Scott, Charles Dickens, George Eliot, and William Thackeray.

They turned from study of the French Revolution and that country's writers to the American Revolutionary period, the war's causes and consequences. Gratified to discover women who'd had important roles in their country's history, they included Margaret Fuller and Julia Ward Howe in their curriculum, acknowledging Howe as the epitome of woman's progress through the ages. They agreed she combined the virtues of their mothers' contemporaries and the ability of theirs.

Finding it exciting to transcend their daily round of cleaning kerosene lamps and struggling with the woodstove, the women wanted the same boost for their children. Patiently they continued to collect volumes of Longfellow, Whittier, Washington Irving, Emerson, Cooper—books they themselves were reading—for the low bookshelves in the little Dunton Avenue living room where the Shepard sisters waited with a smile for the children.

3.
The Library Spirit

Hot baked potatoes at their feet, carriage robes pulled up to their chins, jingling bells ringing in their ears, families rode behind their eager horses up snow-packed Euclid Avenue to the entrance of the Daniel Drapers' handsome red brick home set back from the street just east of Dryden. It was a holiday party at the turn of the century.

Emily Draper was a distinguished hostess, Hillside Farm a mecca for friends and relatives, and an invitation to spend an evening there an entree to congeniality and urbanity.

Daughter of that same Peter Bradley for whom the town was briefly named and who built the Shepards' home, Emily Draper came as a bride to Hillside Farm and soon made her mark on the village. After she had joined the Presbyterian Church, she began a lifetime of decorating the altar there

Emily Draper

22

with choice flowers from her garden. "Her white blossoms have adorned the bride and are laid on the caskets of the dead," a contemporary account read.

Residents on Euclid can remember her trudging down their street early on Sunday mornings, laden with splendid bouquets of cut flowers for the altar of the church. Then she would be seen hiking back, to get ready for Sunday morning service.

She'd spent five years at Wheaton College, graduated in 1864, and taught school one year before she married Daniel Draper. According to her contemporaries, her family and her school were responsible for helping her develop her "fine executive ability," her "mind of unusual strength," and her education "of rare breadth and depth."

Emily Draper was one of the five women invited by Elizabeth Walker, with Nellie Noyes (Best), Mrs. Daniel Fast, Mrs. George Fleming, and Mrs. Milton Goodfellow, to be the first reading circle. When Elizabeth Walker left town, Emily Draper became the group's "honored president and leading spirit," and in time, advisor and president emeritus. "It may be truthfully said that to her indomitable courage, perseverence and endurance, the club owed its many years of usefulness," a newspaper story read.

Her quick sympathy and ready tact were legendary. Her contemporaries considered her the mainspring of the Literary Society, the Chautauqua Circle, the woman's club. "She made the wheels go round." A friend who claimed wide acquaintance stated that never in all her life had she known a woman "who was endowed with more of the graces essential to the moulding of a perfect life and I am prepared to give as my opinion that no woman in that locality has ever done as much as Mrs. Draper in moulding the lives and character of the rising generation."

Emily's son Cyrus was the only veterinarian in the area, traveling as far as Itasca to treat ailing cows. Against one wall of his study in the Draper home he kept a museum cabinet which fascinated the fortunate children allowed in to see his collection of stuffed raccoons, owls, minks, and skinny yellow weasels with sharp eyes.

The beginnings of the woman's club library came under Emily Draper's supervision, and she instituted annual library days at Hillside Farm. All the club members were invited to gather at the Drapers' frame farmhouse, and later their red brick home, set amidst one hundred and twenty acres of meadow, garden and orchard. The apples were free to anyone who would pick them, the flowers decorated the walls "on every festal occasion whether in church, hall, or school house." The hospitality was available to "rich and poor, high and low, young and old," and not least to the women of the club who came bearing books on library days.

The women walked out Euclid Avenue, or road in carriages, to library days, passing Klehm's elm tree farm on the south side of the gravel road (Eastwood today) and the fields on the north where the Chapman boys caught the minks that Dr. Draper had stuffed and displayed in his museum cabinet. Books under arm, or quarters in pocket, the women anticipated the elegant spread that Emily Draper and her daughter-in-law Louise were preparing for them.

Whether it was to their Christmas galas when sleigh after sleigh pulled up to drop off excited guests, or to the summer "library days," the Drapers welcomed all their guests in their big front hall and the handsome rooms beyond. The women who contributed their books (or their quarters) to the library day collections concurred with their contemporary Augustine Birrell that "libraries are not made; they grow." They had the sense that they were in the throes of creation, that

24

Banta Family sleigh

they were making a library grow, as they sipped lemonade under the Drapers' elms, far out in the country in a day when the village pretty much petered out at Euclid and Belmont.

The quarter contribution was not ungenerous. Annual club dues were fifty cents, but they had recently been only twenty-five. Around the turn of the century a man who made ten cents an hour could buy a two-story house, without furnace or indoor plumbing, to be sure, if he was handy and thrifty. Twenty-five cents was two-and-one-half-hours wages for the moderately paid head of house, a tidy donation to the common weal of Arlington Heights.

The returns the women experienced on their subsidy were great because they had a sense that they were bearing, in Thomas Carlyle's words, "all that mankind has done,

25

thought, gained or been . . . in magic preservation in the pages" of the books they cradled under their arms as they promenaded out Euclid to the Drapers' red brick manor.

Book by book, quarter by quarter, they were augmenting the little pool of books that began with the *Autobiography of Benjamin Franklin.* From 150 volumes in 1894, when the Shepards opened their living room to the first patrons, the library expanded in fourteen years to 750 volumes, plus many magazines.

The women grandly excused Effie Shepard from paying her dues to the woman's club and allowed her to keep certain of the fines. She collected $28.45 during the fourteen years she welcomed readers into her living room two days every week, $2.03 a year.

Even with library days and librarians who volunteered their services, however, there was never enough money, never enough books. There weren't even enough seats for the audience when the woman's club sponsored a fund-raiser for the library in 1904.

Some of the guests who had paid their quarters (fifteen cents for children) in advance could not be seated at the Queen Esther Cantata at Arlington Hall that fall. Because they had come to see their friends and neighbors perform, the disappointed guests were promised a second showing, the week after Thanksgiving. In the note of thanks to the local paper, Elinore Haynes, corresponding secretary, called attention to the highly efficient corps of singers under the director, Mr. John V. Whiting, and the handsome sum added to the free library fund of the woman's club.

The money collected went directly for books just as the funds raised at the skit, "Deestrict Skule," and Dr. Lake's lecture, "What Shall We Do with Our Girls?" had done.

Steadily the library added books and bookshelves. The

Library Committee allowed five dollars to buy a bookcase in 1907 when fourteen new books were purchased. The committee, which over the years included faithful workers like Josephine Allen, Hattie McElhose, Mae Muller (teacher of one of the town's famous Sunday school classes), and Nellie Best, whose name became synonymous with the library, continued to levy a quarter a year donation for books and to nudge the library project toward greater volume and efficiency.

The women rejoiced that their efforts were rewarded. Yet their bonus was the aggravation of making some decision about what to do next. Emily Draper, Elizabeth Sigwalt, Effie Shepard, and Hattie Farwell were asked to serve on a committee to work up a solution to the problem of their success.

It was years in coming. It was one thing to collect books. It was another to find a home for them. It was only when school superintendent F. J. Blair issued an edict that all school buildings should be open for educational uses that the women sensed a breakthrough. Maude Castle, the president in 1908, deputized a committee to go to the grammar school board and ask them for a home for the hundreds of books that the women in the club had been amassing for several decades.

Mr. J. V. Whiting, who'd already played a part in raising funds for the library, was chairman of the board at the time, serving with Charles Taege, L. B. Wayman, F. H. Sieburg, Louis Roehler, and George K. Volz. They were sympathetic to the women's problem of overflowing books at the Shepards', and to the children's good which would attend on a library convenient to them.

The board agreed that a door should be cut through double walls in the old high school in order to make space for the several hundred books the women were bringing. A recitation room would be given up.

Superintendent Blair cited the North School addition as the first public library in a public school building outside of Chicago.

It was July 20, 1909, before the change was made. After the books, which she had lovingly pressed on visiting readers in her home, were moved to the club room in the old building of North School, Effie Shepard wrote a poignant letter to the *Cook County Herald.* She told how she had served as librarian without salary for fourteen years and how she had indexed the principal subjects in eighty-four bound magazines and "tried to do (her) duty faithfully giving no cause for complaint."

Miss Effie harbored the hope that now she would be hired as a paid librarian, expressing her regret that she was obliged to resign because she had enjoyed keeping the library. "I wish I might be elected to the office again with a fair compensation, a dollar a day is what it is worth, giving two days a week for the care of the library."

Evidently the club members were not able to consider Effie's "need of earning a livelihood." When the library was established at North School, the library committee took responsibility for running it during open hours and, as Miss Effie said in her letter, "clearing up and putting in order."

It was a prodigious job for women who were full-time homemakers and mothers. The library committee changed from year to year but there were stalwart faithfuls like Nellie Best who identified themselves with that aspect of the woman's club. Nellie, an artistic woman who took music lessons from Florenz Ziegfeld, was the purchasing agent. She watched for the yearly sales at Chicago bookstores and rode the train downtown, armed with funds and lists. She'd come home laden, carrying all her treasures in bags, to save the cartage costs.

For Lucy and Effie Shepard a letter was published in the *Cook County Herald* quoting the unanimous resolution passed at the November 3, 1909, meeting. "I move that a hearty vote of thanks be given to the Misses Lucy and Effie Shepard in appreciation of services rendered the club in furnishing room and efficiently caring for the library for fourteen years."

The library in the school was popular with the children. It was convenient for them. Adults had to be appealed to with reminders that there were many excellent books for them on the shelves in North School.

Nellie Best bought books for grown-up readers as well as children, but the adults didn't rely on books for entertainment and information the way children did. The committee tried to entice them. "It is not crowded in summer and there are lots of good books there free."

Still there were more children skipping in after classes for *The Five Little Peppers* than adults making special trips for Jacob Riis' *The Making of An American*.

Woman's club members who took their turns behind the check-out desk in the little office in North School had what one of their presidents called the "library spirit," a real and driving force "meaning personal sacrifice and the hardest of work," according to Vera Noyes, interviewed years later.

"There wasn't a college graduate among us in those days," she recalled, not entirely correctly, when she was the club's oldest member, "but we were determined to improve ourselves, to read and discuss, and most of all to make better homes and better lives for our children."

Club minutes during those years reflect the members' impatience at the lack of money for books. Besides library days at the Drapers' and solicitations for books members were no longer reading, the club women threw bazaars to raise money for Nellie Best's forays on the North Western to Chicago's bookshops.

They organized rummage sales, bake sales, ice cream socials, parcel post parties, and white elephant sales, as well as a stereoptical and motion picture show by William Leffingwell. One of the parcel post parties brought in $41 and a bazaar realized $145. Some of the affairs provided small profit for the amount of energy expended. The women were exultant when the Woman's Civic League contributed $334.68 to the fund.

They were equally pleased when Willie Weber and Ralphie Nehls produced a magic lantern show and donated the profits—money for one book. This showed the children wanted a library enough so that they were willing to expend time and effort, just as their collecting magazines and newspapers for the fund did.

The N. M. Banta family donated a large number of chil-

Second North School building

dren's books, a set of George Eliot's works, and a set of McCauley's History of England. Banta was to figure largely in the library's next stage of development.

At first the schoolhouse library was open on Tuesday from 4 to 5:30 p.m. and on Friday from 4 to 9:30 p.m. As more students packed North School and the superintendent moved into the library room, the library was crowded over to the upstairs hall in the new building. That's where Elinor Hackbarth, whose family moved to Arlington Heights in 1917, remembers the library—in the corridor outside her fourth grade classroom.

There the faithful committee members greeted the children, helped them choose books, contended with dust and lack of privacy, rebound the books when necessary, and added to the collection as intelligently and rapidly as they could.

Some young patrons found Nellie Best somewhat domineering in the days when the library took up several bookcases between the first and second floors of the old school building. "If you wanted to take a book out, Mrs. Best would ask you who it was for. And if it was for you and not for your mother, and if she thought it was unsuitable, then she wouldn't let you have it."

The women were particular about the books they bought, and the books they lent. Their high standards extended to the fund-raisers they sponsored. On May 18, 1910, a state senator who had spent a good part of his life researching Abraham Lincoln spoke at Arlington Hall. Just as a library could grow through patience and persistence, he told the audience, so individuals in this free country have an opportunity to rise "if ambition is awakened and they are willing to work patiently and persistently.

"Virtue and judicious labor bring their own reward," the Honorable Louis J. Pierson said, neatly undergirding the women's hope that they were helping the village children to lead lives of that very virtue and judicious labor.

Not all of the club women had the same tenacity, but the library committee—Elinore Haynes, Nellie Best, Edith Jenkinson, Ella Taylor, Mary Dyas, and Mrs. Fred Lorenzen—worked "long and faithfully, giving out books, taking them home to be mended and making the best of a difficult situation."

Buoyed by the notion that they were not only giving the public a love of reading which, as English novelist Anthony Trollope said, "lasts when all other pleasures fade," the women had the sense that they were creating a sentiment throughout the community in favor of enlarging the scope of the library. They appeared at their appointed places every Tuesday afternoon from 2 to 4 p.m.

By 1915 the members could no longer count how many newspapers they had tied, how many aprons they had bought at bazaars, how many cups of lemonade they had drunk, how many servings of double chocolate cake they had eaten, how many house dresses they had donated to rummage sales, to accumulate the one thousand volumes that could be checked out of the North School library those Tuesday afternoons.

They realized that books were being taken into many homes where the parents had never seen an illustrated English story book. According to Nellie Best, these parents saw "how their children enjoyed these books." Some of the library sponsors awoke to the fact that it might be possible to carry a vote in the village authorizing an .0018 tax per $100 of property evaluation to maintain a public library.

The first youngsters had started going to Miss Lucy and Miss Effie to borrow books in 1894. Now many of them were old enough to vote. The library sponsors had been building up good will for years, long enough to have created some sympathetic voters.

The library had now been in North School since 1909, open to the public every Tuesday afternoon. Busy readers checked out three thousand books a year in spite of the fact that the library room was crowded and inconvenient. According to a newspaper report, "some of the little-called-for books are kept in a closet for lack of space. Sometimes the school children crowd the room to overflowing. Then it is hard for the children to find books they want and the members of the library committee who give their time and labor to this work are worn out at the end of the afternoon."

The women didn't complain. Their only published grumble was concerning the number of adult readers. This is one of the factors that kept them investigating new locations. In 1918 they found a little building they considered ideal for their purposes. The Bergman office on the east side of the railroad park at State Road and Davis Street was being sold for a modest price, fifteen hundred dollars, a fraction of the cost of building its two stories and basement containing a shower.

Between them, the Arlington Heights Woman's Club and the Woman's Civic League, another local group interested in a public library, had seven hundred dollars toward the purchase price. Once they had the consent of the railroad the women intended to go to the public for the additional eight hundred dollars for a building which would house the library as well as the two clubs.

Their constituencies did not share their leaders' enthusiasm for a building on leased land for which they did not have the full purchase price on hand. "We might have to move it," members said. "It's poor business to own a building on leased land as the present low price of this beautiful little building proves." Besides, they added, "during wartime is no time to spend individual cash for anything other than winning the war."

So the library committee marched back to their North School hall library and continued to contend with the dust and the bother, quietly rejoicing in the 2,717 books they lent that year of 1918, including those for adults on a special shelf of non-fiction.

They bought twenty-seven new books that year, a little over two a month. Seventy-three were donated. They collected $10.98 from the five and ten cents shelf and received a dollar and a half for old books.

Any suitable library quarters were still almost a decade in the future.

4.
"Let's Get Some Women On The Board"

Like some local social groups who had their beer delivered to the back door so they could keep their temperance image, conservative Arlington Heights had a flip side in the twenties.

This time the national movement affecting the village was not uplifting like Chautauqua. It was an anti-Prohibition lawlessness. Many villagers did not cotton to the Volstead Act forbidding the manufacture, sale, or transportation of beverages which contained one-half of one per centum or more of alcohol by volume.

One witness claimed there was no change in town when Prohibition took hold at midnight, June 30, 1919. "The same drunks rolled out of the same taverns." And continued to do so.

Speakeasies were handy to downtown businesses.

The village of three thousand was ricocheting off a wall of change, not only the restrictions on drinking. The first high school building was born in controversy in 1923. The first three-story building shaded downtown streets. Helen Siemro got the first permanent in town on the stage at the Arlington Theater.

As the last blacksmith shops closed their doors, the first bookies opened theirs.

Stills abounded. People who had been used to brewing

their own liquor continued to do it. Others learned how. The more professional cut holes in floors to make room for larger stills. The set-up at Thomas and Belmont was in operation twenty-four hours a day until the neighbors, annoyed by the relentless rattle of trucks pulling in night and day, called the police. Notorious Roger Touhy bought wine from local wine-makers. Gangster Babyface Nelson was shot in a nearby farm driveway.

When the racetrack opened in the middle of the decade there were merchants who lost their businesses making bets or taking them. They found out, too late, that standing behind a counter all day, however stodgy and tiring, was an infinitely more reliable way of supporting a wife and kids.

Police were busy. They chopped up stills and poured moonshine down sewers. Federal agents found whiskey, homebrew, wine, and gin.

The real contestants against the downturn of village life were not the police armed with axes and arrest warrants, but those villagers who were determined to serve and improve the community they lived in. They were many. Even then a group that stood out was the Tri-Sigmas, a student group at the First Methodist Church.

Sunday schools always had a substantial effect on Arlington Heights, their students, and their churches. People in their eighties today still identify themselves as part of Mae Muller's Sunday school class at the Presbyterian Church seventy years ago. Few groups, however, can have had the civic impact of John Beaty's Tri-Sigma group at the Methodist church in the twenties.

John Y. Beaty was as respectful of the common good of his village as mob-related still operators were disrespectful of it. Beaty taught young people at the Methodist Church that they could change their town for the better—and it was their responsibility to do so. He believed they could do it. Because he believed in them they believed in themselves.

Beaty worked as book editor at Popular Mechanics Press in Chicago. Born in Finchford, Iowa, in 1854, he had taught journalism at the University of Wisconsin and edited Luther Burbank's autobiography and several agricultural magazines before settling in Arlington Heights.

Beaty's openness to new directions, his interested attention to village affairs, his respect for young persons, and his eagerness to see them develop self-worth through achievement affected Tri-Sigma members. Along with Mr. Beaty they wanted to have an effect on their village.

They were able to do it.

Like the pioneers in that original Chautauqua summer program for Sunday school teachers that had started the whole movement, the Tri-Sigma group wanted to serve their

Methodist Church, 1925

community in "improving the health of persons living here, in increasing education, in providing wholesome entertainment, and increasing religious service."

The members were largely, but not entirely, Methodist. Anyone who shared their ideals was welcome to the parties and all the business meetings, anyone who was willing to put his or her "shoulder to the wheel and push in the same direction."

Tri-Sigma directions pointed to:

A community library for Arlington Heights.

Organized outdoor games for the whole community.

A night school for foreigners.

Appreciative as they were of the woman's club library in the hall at North School where many of them had "read everything they could get their hands on," members of Tri-Sigma could see that if reading is to the mind what exercise is to the body, as essayist Richard Steele assured them it was, then the village needed a library with a reading room which could be open at hours convenient enough so that everyone could participate in those mental calisthenics.

The *Cook County Herald* showed its sympathy to the Tri-Sigmas' lofty aims by donating weekly space for write-ups about their projects, particularly their library project. Writer Beaty, with the occasional help of others like Tri-Sigma president Noble Puffer who went on to become superintendent of Cook County schools, filled the space week after week, preaching reading, libraries, mental growth as well as physical.

By October, 1925, suggestion was already being made that there might be a patron in the downtown area willing to donate accommodations for a reading room that could be open in the evenings to the reading public.

Even as they agitated for a new library reading room, the

38

Tri-Sigmas continued to give credit to the women of the club who had already been working toward a town library for over thirty years. They commended the women for the fifteen hundred books they had already collected, and the 120 which were loaned out each week.

At the same time the Tri-Sigmas could see that that effort was too limited. A large children's section and a "number of modern novels by the better authors" were all very well. But they couldn't make a library when it was only open on Tuesdays from 2 to 4 p.m., the year round.

Minds needed more exercise than that.

Gradually the Tri-Sigmas persuaded villagers that each of them had a personal investment in the library project. Or should have. The more each had invested in money and interest, the more each would be interested in the library's growth and effectiveness. The Tri-Sigmas pointed out that if only the businesses were approached for support, and not the citizenry, that the villagers "won't be nearly so interested and the library won't be used as much as it should."

Their investigation turned up an Illinois law providing that the village board must levy a two mill tax for library support in response to the proper petition. Eager Tri-Sigmas made up their minds that those petitions would be made available. Their theory was that anything good can be done if enough folks want it done. Their job was to see that folks wanted it done. Already they were suggesting that people with particular interests could endow library collections in their specialty.

About this time the president of the Peoples State Bank, which was located east of Dunton where Campbell and Davis met at "the point"—surely a central location—let it be known that the large airy and light room on the second floor of the bank was going to be devoted to the welfare of the community.

To the young persons who were eyeing Palatine's new rudimentary library in the rear of a downtown store, the idea of a handsome room at the heart of the village for an "education center used by everyone who can visit Arlington Heights" sounded perfect. "You'd be surprised," the weekly column in the *Herald* read, "at the wonderful good you and your children can get from books."

The Tri-Sigmas had discovered by this time that they would have to give a sixty-day notice to get their library tax proposal on the election ballot in April, 1926. They were impatient. "Let's all chip in just a little, say fifty cents, or a dollar apiece, and get the library started right away."

They were feeling their oats because their projects were coming to life. High school Superintendent V. I. Brown had declared his interest in the night school for foreigners and offered his services to set up a program "that will be worthwhile for those in Arlington Heights who want to learn the language and ways of our country." The night school was for residents who wished to learn to speak, read, and write in the English language, and for those who wished to prepare themselves for taking out their naturalization papers.

The Tri-Sigmas' playground program was swinging along. They had employed and paid two playground instructors entirely out of their funds and benefitted sixty children in the summer. They even arranged a camping trip for the boys. Community games were also under way.

When the Tri-Sigmas started library solicitation, they asked villagers to contribute whatever amount they could to a fund that would be used to operate a library until such time as a community tax could be levied to support the library.

"Give as liberally as you can. We certainly ought to have

five hundred dollars to run the library for a year. If we get more, we can make a larger library." Tri-Sigmas planned to invite each contributor to a public meeting to elect a board of directors who would employ a librarian and select a location.

They were high on community participation. They wanted each villager to "own" the library. "Even if you only own fifty cents or a dollar's worth, you will take more interest in the project, and will use it more. Don't hesitate, then, to give even if your gift is small."

The Tri-Sigmas wanted to ban trashy stories from the library and to boost inspirational literature. They cited a story about a boy who read about an inventor and devised articles useful to thousands of folk, and a mother who appreciated how fortunate her children were after reading about a slum family. They noted a father who spent more time with his son after he read a book for dads.

To buttress their argument that books help a person build character (and therefore there should be a library), the Tri-Sigmas emphasized the usefulness of books in keeping off the streets people who wouldn't know what to do with themselves without books and magazines. "They would be getting into mischief."

To get those people the right books, the weekly *Herald* columnist for the Tri-Sigmas warned that electing a good library board is the safeguard. The columnist was specific. Board members should have high Christian ideals. They should have the interests of the patrons at heart. They should own property in Arlington Heights so that they would have a personal stake in making this the "best small-town library in the state of Illinois."

The columnist went on to suggest that the overburdened members of the school board and village board should not double as library board members, as they were already doing on those other boards. One way to make sure that the members were not on boards already was to choose women. "Let's get some women on the library board. And let's get women who know something about library work."

Aiming to become the most helpful organization in Arlington Heights, the Tri-Sigmas took to heart Mr. Beaty's exhortation that Tri-Sigmas should not only stand for the three S's (study, service, and sociability), but also for the three C's (character, church, and community).

Like the woman's club before them, the Tri-Sigmas tried raising funds for community projects by putting on a play. The cast included John Beaty, the Tri-Sigma teacher, and his wife.

Play patrons knew in advance that library pledge cards would be handed out, to be picked up by the ushers between acts. Playgoers were going to be asked to pledge on a deferred payment plan. Tri-Sigmas did not want to handle the money but they wanted it available at definite times: when the library board was elected, two months after the library opened, and six months after the library opened. With their contributions patrons would be showing that they wanted Arlington Heights to have a creditable community library for the free use of everyone in the community.

A suggested donation of five dollars would buy from two to five good books. "Looking at it from a selfish standpoint, your five dollars will be worth about fifty times five dollars to you personally, because it will place at your disposal for free use, about five hundred dollars worth of books."

Books meant progress, according to Tri-Sigmas. "Even today, among some peoples where books are not read, there is no progress except as a little is absorbed from men who come in from the outside world where books are available."

5.
"No Advance Without Dissension"

Arlington Heights' population may have been only slowly creeping toward the five thousand mark in the twenties, but to the people in the surrounding countryside it was the metropolis.

Always there was a village contingent who lived a good part of their lives in Chicago. They shopped at Marshall Field's. They worked in the Loop. They took the train into the city for a concert, perhaps, or ice cream at Kranz' across State Street from Field's, or hazelnut torte at Henrici's on Randolph where politicians hung out.

For every person drawn toward the big city for the enhancement of their lives, there were a dozen on farms up Arlington Heights Road (then State Road), out Kirchhoff, and along Algonquin and Foundry Roads, that looked to Arlington Heights for an evening out.

Often that big night on the town meant a church supper. Many of the churches provided them. In summer they were often held on Sunday afternoon. They were a prodigy of work. Later, women wondered how they had ever done it, cleaned all those turkeys and kept them in ice water. Peeled all those potatoes. Prepared all those biscuits. In some churches the SOS went out and twenty women would be assigned to arrive, cakes in hand.

The women were wonderful organizers. They'd have a

crew for the salad table, another for the steam table, a potato crew. The leader would assess the size of the crowd arriving each night, and dash uptown for extra supplies if necessary. One supervisor remembers running short of potatoes for a Methodist dinner and asking the Greek restaurant owner in town if he couldn't help out. "I stood on that pavement what seemed an eternity," she recalls, "waiting for him to fill the kettle. Then I dropped it out of my hand, the potatoes I needed so badly lining the curb at my feet. I was ready to cry."

However exhausting a drain they were on the organizers, the church suppers represented sociability and a rare night away from the woodstove and dishpan to the mothers of farm families. They were summer's high old times.

Plays and concerts in Arlington Heights found the same kind of ready audience. For most villagers and farmers a train ride to Chicago for entertainment was out of the question. But when they had an opportunity to take the horse and buggy out to carry their families to a play at Arlington Hall, spending a quarter for the adults, perhaps, and fifteen cents for the children—and almost always with the promise that the money would go to a good cause—the populace was easily persuaded. The tickets would be sold out as quickly as farmers could urge their "old Dobbins" to Rubner's Drug Store.

The tickets were often gone before the first night of the performance, and more than once the *Cook County Herald* noted a number of ticket-holders who were disappointed to find there were no seats even though they had paid for them in advance.

Safety First was this kind of success. When they read in the paper that these "are the players who have pleased you before. They have all had experience and it certainly seems that they will do their best in this play, for every character has an opportunity to make much out of his part," local play-goers planned to buy their tickets as soon as possible. Fifty tickets were immediately sold to out-of-town theater-goers.

They were promised that the Tri-Sigmas' *Safety First* at Arlington High School, with the Arlington Heights high school orchestra playing for the first time, was funnier than Harold Lloyd's *Safety First*. "Oh, you've got a lot of surprises in store for you."

The director of the high school orchestra who handled her violin "as easily as most of us handle a knife and fork" trained the young players to back up the Tri-Sigma's comedic routines. The cast spent long hours rehearsing, buoyed up by anticipation of their first night and their expectation that the performance would elicit solid contributions for their library project.

John Beaty was to make the pitch. The sponsor of the Tri-Sigma group announced to the group gathered to see *Safety First* that it was true that the people of Arlington Heights were going to provide themselves with a community library. "Subscriptions have already been received that assure the success of the plan, and I know from your smiling faces that those of you here are going to subscribe liberally."

Beaty cited Tri-Sigma member Vera McElhose as the first to make a pledge, and assured the audience that the Tri-Sigmas would contribute a liberal amount themselves as soon as the expenses for the play were paid.

From the start the Tri-Sigmas emphasized that they were not working for a library that would serve a small elite. Beaty made that point forcibly. "This will be a community library in every sense of the word. It will be free to everyone in the community whether they have contributed to it or not. It will be owned by the community. It will be maintained by the

45

community until such time as the voters authorize a tax to support it."

Just as they were assiduous in stressing the community nature of the library, Beaty and the Tri-Sigmas continually acknowledged the thousands of woman-hours and hundreds of dollars that the members of the Arlington Heights Woman's Club had devoted to the advancement of a community library. Complimenting the woman's club, Beaty pointed to the years they had provided the library in the school. "I do not suppose that half of those who are here know that this library gives out over one hundred books a week. This is done in spite of many handicaps that have been very discouraging to the library committee."

Beaty told the audience that the women had never had any help with their library. "Surely it is time now that they be given some assistance. We should not expect one organization to provide the town with an adequate library and reading room."

Within the week of *Safety First,* the directors of the Peoples State Bank agreed to sacrifice the profit for the room over the bank that had been used by the Red Cross during World War I. They would charge the library a minimal rent of sixteen dollars to cover the cost of the heat and light.

This was the location the Tri-Sigmas had set their hearts on. The bank was a flatiron building in the little island formed in the angle of the North Western tracks and the east-west street. Trees softened the view across Davis. At the confluence of Davis, Campbell, and Evergreen, a large circular watering trough made a natural stopping place. Stores, station, and hotels were steps away. The second floor room was commodious, with plenty of space for chairs and tables.

Now the Tri-Sigmas put their shoulders to the wheel in earnest. One of their members pledged a handsome $8, in four installments. Overall, the group members gave $125. Pledges signed at *Safety First* amounted to $181.75.

The Tri-Sigmas had first estimated that the library expenses for the first year would be five hundred dollars. Now the group speculated that one thousand dollars might be a more appropriate budget. They could set their sights higher because of the encouraging public support and the bank officers' generous offer of their upper room.

Their expectations were fulfilled. That first week the total contribution went up to $250. The list of pledges, with Vera McElhose's name still leading the roster, was printed in the *Herald.*

Most people were generously supportive of the Tri-Sigmas' effort. Gradually they heard enough criticism, however, to let a little air out of their balloon. They had said from the start

Peoples Bank, library site, 1926-1930

that they were not interested in getting any credit for their community efforts. But there was sufficient undercover comment to force them to reiterate their assurance that they were not seeking personal glory, or credit for their church or their society.

No advancement ever came to Arlington Heights without dissension. When Al Volz was mayor in the early part of the century he complained that he had to get everything past those "tight-fisted Dutchman farmers." Mayor John Walsh, fifty years later, remarked on the bitterness with which every neighborhood countered change—whatever it was.

It's hardly a surprise that criticism of the Tri-Sigmas' plan caused a grumbling undercurrent.

It was hinted, for instance, that the church connection handicapped the library effort. "Why should there be competition between churches?" the *Herald* columnist asked in the Christmas 1925 issue. "We don't think there should be. We are all working for the same good cause. We think just as much of you if you belong to another organization as we would if you belonged to ours—that is, if you are loyal to that organization."

Adding that "we are glad when other churches enlarge their influence," the Tri-Sigmas made a last plea not to be given credit for the library project. "We don't want credit—we want a community that is constantly improving. That's what we want and so do you. Let's work together to get it."

By January 8 the fund was up to $325. "Every additional dollar means an additional book," Tri-Sigmas maintained, urging anyone who had not done so to secure a pledge at Zimmer's store or Rubner's Drugs, fill it out, and leave it at the store. The largest personal pledge so far was $25, the smallest 25 cents, the average $6. In addition to their $125 in personal pledges, the Tri-Sigmas as a group pledged $50 to

48

undergird their belief that "nothing else will help Arlington Heights quite so much right now as a good library."

Countering unspecified criticisms about the library project, the *Herald* columnist made three clarifications: 1.) that the Tri-Sigma efforts were not going to be "spasmodic," 2.) that the previous criticism had led to more converts, and 3.) that the Tri-Sigmas were not writing to the Carnegie Institute for help at this time because they were not planning on erecting a building, only renting a room.

Tri-Sigmas had made personal pleas for each of their seventy-eight contributions. In spite of their repeated appeals that two hundred contributors could handle the library's budget for a year, no one had actually gone to Rubner's store, or Zimmer's, picked up a pledge and signed up.

During Library Week the Tri-Sigmas tried a new tactic. They wrote every person listed in the telephone directory, asking that they return stamped postcards with pledges.

By this time the Tri-Sigmas had worked out a proposed constitution based on suggestions made by the library extension division of the state library at Springfield. The name chosen was The Arlington Heights Community Library Association. The purpose: the building up and maintaining of a free public library for Arlington Heights and the territory adjoining it.

They meant that this temporary organization would be supplanted by a library board elected by the voters of the community once this original organization should have got the library off the ground.

Board members would be elected at the time of the spring election in Arlington and they would be responsible for raising money and supervision of book purchase, library finances, library grounds committee, and the administration.

Then the Tri-Sigmas' work would be done.

6.
The First Board

Every town appropriates part of the national myth for its own. To many people in Arlington Heights it seemed natural to identify with Abraham Lincoln.

Villagers could tell stories of forebears who rose from log cabins and hardscrabble farms to lives of literacy, cultivation, and service. Sagas of pioneering struggles were as familiar and numerous as the arrowheads Budge Kellogg collected by the thousands, or Mrs. Dunton's recollections of Indians camping in downtown Arlington Heights.

Nathaniel Moore Banta's story was vintage Americana, rags to riches in one generation. He had a direct connection to the California Gold Rush through his father who had taken off to seek his fortune in the California hills in 1849. Disappointed, Henry Banta had returned to Rensselaer, Indiana, married Nathaniel Moore Banta's mother and settled into farming.

But visions of gold nuggets still danced in his head. When Moore Banta was ten years old, his father turned his face—and his hopes—once again to the great West. Taking the three youngest of their ten children, including Moore, the Bantas climbed into their covered wagon and set out to seek treasure where eggs could cost a fortune, a dollar apiece.

Henry Banta set his sights on a fortuitous windfall. Again, his hopes were crushed. The family animals had pulled the wagon belly through the mud only so far as southwestern Missouri when Henry Banta sickened and died, abandoning his wife and three young children to the frustration of his dream and the outcome of his folly.

That spirit of gallantry and determination which characterized Nathaniel Moore Banta when Arlington Heights knew him after his arrival in 1900 already showed in the spunky little boy who always recalled his Missouri days fondly: "We were so happy but so poor."

Already capable, Banta worked on farms to help his mother and sisters until the family could make its way back to Indiana when he was sixteen. By now he was qualified to run a farm, and it looked as if Moore Banta had found his life's work.

But when the father of a friend asked him if he wouldn't like to go to college, Banta realized that he "wanted an education more than anything in the world." In spite of the fact that his schooling had been sporadic, that he had no high school diploma, Banta was allowed to register at Valparaiso University in northwest Indiana. He continued to manage farms in the summer, supporting his family, until he completed his degree. Then he found a job selling rare book bindings which gave him the opportunity to travel.

He came to Arlington Heights in 1900 as eighth grade teacher and principal at North School after he had changed careers and taught in Indiana, and eight years in Niles Center, Illinois. Grown men remembered in the sixties how frightened they were to be sent to the principal in Banta's day because a leather strap could be used to keep obstreperous lads in line.

By the time he arrived in Arlington Heights, Banta had taken additional courses at the University of Chicago, at the Berlitz School, and at the Soper School of Oratory. He brought a rich knowledge of the world to the little village which didn't yet have a paved road or a storm sewer to keep

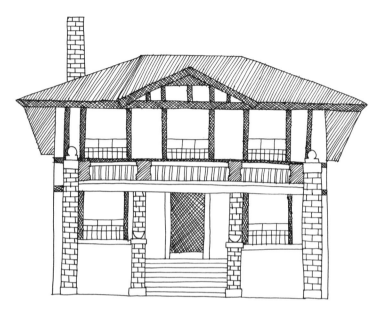

Banta House, Euclid and Vail, 1906

local creeks from overflowing when there was a heavy rain.

He found his bride in Arlington Heights, the daughter of "Pop" Muller, the owner of one of the town's earliest businesses, the "Pop Factory," at Vail and Fremont which is now part of the Arlington Heights Historical Museum complex.

A measure of the man Nathanial Moore Banta is the home he built in 1906. (Like his father-in-law's home and factory, that house is a part of the museum complex today.) On the lot at Euclid and Vail he bought for one thousand dollars from Pop Muller, Banta envisioned a prairie style home, the style popularized by Frank Lloyd Wright.

Banta's enterprising and talented mother-in-law, who began

laying out her own plans for her daughter's and son-in-law's home as soon as the sale of the lot was completed, was as surprised as the rest of the village when Banta brought in architect Ralph Abell from Elgin to design his family a home with horizontal lines and wide overhanging eaves, a living room instead of the usual two parlors, kitchen cupboards instead of a pantry, and striking stained glass windows. Banta's travels had widened his visual imagination beyond the traditional farmhouse-type architecture and dated Queen Annes which could be seen up and down every village street.

Young people flocked to the Bantas to enjoy his daughter Betty's parties, the music from the new Victrola, and the dancing. Their voices would carry through the night as they swung their lanterns, making their way home through the snowdrifts after a social evening.

Banta switched from school teaching to book editing. He managed the publication department of A. Flanagan, book publishers, in Chicago. Linking his knowledge of books and his way with children, Banta began publishing his own children's books in 1905. By 1927 he had written twenty-two books of his own, as well as edited eleven volumes of *Nature Neighbors.*

"I was a great disappointment to my father because I didn't like fairy stories," Banta's daughter recalled in later years. "He wrote quite a few of them." Actually, Banta originated the highly fanciful Brownies stories very popular in the 1920s. *The Brownie Primer* appeared in 1905, followed by *Brownies and the Goblins.* The last of the series, *Brownies in the Greenwood,* did not come out until 1927.

Nathaniel Moore Banta's whole life was involved with books. He was going to be a natural choice when the first library board looked for a president.

That election was months in the future as the year turned

Ten Little Brownie Men

to 1926. That winter the Tri-Sigmas continued to cajole the townspeople into the idea of a library, advising the electorate—those who had pledged, in this case—to choose "men and women who have such work on their hearts, who have the time and ideals" to serve on the library board. These people should be selected from all classes, the Tri-Sigmas advised, and "no particular group of people should have more representatives than another."

Having culled their contemporary constitution from the suggestions made by the library extension people, the Tri-Sigmas were ready to signal "go" once the thousand dollars had been collected and the board elected. Their plan was to position the library for operation without delay.

They were hoping for a woman librarian who would bring books to the running shelves, sermons to those looking for inspiration, and good reading to everyone for very little—or no—pay.

Support was growing. Arlington High School, which had its own share of controversy in getting off the ground, responded with an expansive willingness to requests to share its large rooms. The board offered the gymnasium free for affairs that were open to everyone in the high school district.

The Lions Club heartily endorsed the library project in a resolution in which it was recommended that all members subscribe liberally to the fund. The Business Men's Association put library support on its agenda. The Arlington Theater gave forty percent of the receipts the Monday evening it showed *An American Venus,* a "wholesome" picture featuring Fay Lamphier, who had won the Atlantic City Beauty Contest the year before.

A grade school youngster who was persuaded that the library would be a boon for him and his friends burst into Zimmer's store and handed in a dollar that he had earned himself, saying he had "planned to give it to the library without anyone suggesting it to him."

Meanwhile the Tri-Sigmas repeatedly explained that they were collecting the pledges because they could see that the villagers needed to experience the benefits of a library before they would vote a tax to pay for one. After all, villagers had voted down library taxes before.

Tri-Sigmas stressed the notion that the library board would not be publicly elected because there was no authority for an election of a library board until that library tax had been voted.

They tried to make it plain that they were not taking in any of the money. It was all in the form of pledges against the day that there should be a library board, and for the day when the library began to operate.

Right along as they collected their one thousand dollars, quarter by quarter, two dollar pledge after three dollar, but never a one hundred dollar promise to put them over the top in a bound, the Tri-Sigmas were forced to rebut low-key criticism, uneasy murmurings about their plans and organization.

Patiently, John Beaty used the *Cook County Herald* columns to reassure. "We are not sorry that a Methodist organization had done the work on this proposition, but we are sorry that our motive has been misinterpreted by a few."

Yet the Tri-Sigmas could afford to congratulate themselves a little, surely. Their organization not a year old, they were in sight of the election of a library board and the realization of a downtown library. Now the Tri-Sigmas began a house-to-house canvas for pledges and for books. Their enthusiasm was boundless.

By their first birthday in March their plan was coming together. They had completed the subscriptions for the first year's expenses. They had one thousand dollars.

The longed-for culmination was within reach when the meeting to elect a library board was set up for March 29, 1926, in the Village Hall. Anyone who had subscribed any amount whatever was eligible to vote for this first board. That franchise was open to the very last instant. Anyone who came in and made a contribution was welcome to vote.

Tri-Sigmas were still hoping that some of the candidates would be women.

The long-planned-for night arrived. To the one-story Village Hall at Wing Street trooped the jubilant Tri-Sigmas, the playgoers who had pledged at *Safety First,* kids like the boy who'd handed over the dollar he'd earned himself, those who gave to the eager young Tri-Sigmas who had rung their doorbells, and all those who had pledged.

The Tri-Sigmas suggested a slate and encouraged nominations from the floor. They were quietly exultant when their choice as first board president for the Arlington Heights Community Library, a man "whose whole life was involved with books," the author who had donated his own writings to the collection, their former principal, was elected.

Elected with Banta were two women, as the Tri-Sigmas had hoped there would be: Lillian Russell, one of the town's beloved teachers, and Adella T. Guild, a loyal worker at the woman's club library who had recently served as president of the Arlington Heights Woman's Club. John Beaty, sponsor of the Tri-Sigmas; Arthur McElhose, cashier at the Peoples Bank, and Frank J. Sachs rounded out the board.

Their role was to launch a community library in the large sunny room over the Peoples Bank and to commandeer support for the library tax which would be voted on in the April 23 election. Voters were also going to be asked to settle whether they should have a municipal band. Some commentators surmised that the voters would never extend themselves to cover two new enterprises. But Banta was of a more positive mind. He told everyone that he had so much faith in the good judgment of the people of Arlington Heights that there was no doubt in his mind that they would approve.

Banta's board hit the wire with force just as the Tri-Sigmas had hoped they would. In short order they hired Frances Jenkinson as librarian for $2.50 a day and decided that the library should be open on Wednesdays and Saturdays from 2 to 5 p.m., and 7 to 9 p.m. They rented the room over the Peoples Bank for sixteen dollars a month and accepted an offer from the lumber yard managers to make the shelves. They decided on a loan period of two weeks, and a penny a day fine for overdue books.

Less than three weeks after their election the library was opened on April 17, 1926. One hundred books were borrowed the first week. Encouraged, the board authorized twenty-five dollars for expenditures, and funds for one hundred books—not to cost over fifty dollars—on the day the library opened its doors. They already had on their shelves the seven hundred books donated by the villagers.

7.
The First Tax

Lloyd Baldwin went to the library and took down a book from the shelf. He read, "In the library many boys and girls were reading books and magazines. Lloyd asked the librarian who pays for all the books.

" 'The town pays for them,' said the librarian. 'That is why you may borrow books free.' "

That short passage didn't begin to tell the story of toil and endurance and aspiration that brought the Arlington Heights Public Library into existence. But Lloyd Baldwin was not apt to be critical. He was reading about his very own library in a book in which he himself was a very real character.

And there he was in a picture with everyone's favorite librarian, Mrs. Baxter, right in *Story Pictures of Our Neighbors.* Here he was with his sister Jean at the Arlington

Heights sewage treatment plant, and waiting at the Dunton Street railroad crossing for the gates to rise.

Not only were Jean and Lloyd Baldwin in the new book by their neighbor John Yocum Beaty, but also Police Chief Skoog and Fire Chief George Volz and Miss Jackson, the community nurse. There were pictures showing the interiors of the Arlington Bootery, Mors Bakery, Heller Lumber Company, and Gieseke's Drygoods.

Their town was famous.

Just as the library association board boasted two women, Mrs. Guild and Miss Russell, even more remarkably, it harbored two writers among the six members. N. Moore Banta was the author of the Brownie stories, of course. Long-time library advocate John Beaty, the Tri-Sigmas' moderator, also wrote children's books.

Actually, Beaty was editor, lecturer, author, advertising executive, and an ardent student of nature. By 1946 he would have written twenty-one books.

In the spring of 1926 Beaty's book about Jean and Lloyd Baldwin at the Arlington Heights library was still in the future, but the actual library was getting its start in the Peoples Bank building. Beaty was very much one of its godfathers. He'd been responsible for inspiring the Tri-Sigmas, of course, and for most of the columns in the *Cook County Herald* urging a library on the townspeople.

Now he threw himself into the work of the board. He was elected secretary. He was chairperson of the finance and publicity committees—he *was* the publicity committee. He helped catalog the Bobbsey Twin series and the Rootabaga Stories and the Sinclair Lewis novels that the library was now buying. He noted that children were still the more frequent borrowers, as they were at the North School library.

Six days after the library opened on April 17, Arlington

59

Heights voters gathered at the polling place at village hall to decide if they wanted to raise their taxes to support a town library and a town band. There was talk that two referenda were too much to ask, in the light of the institution of a park district just the year before. Others argued that adding a library and a band to the park district would show "the modern progressive spirit existing in the City of Good Neighbors."

The people of the town could see that Banta and his board were making headway in setting up a library. The town was full of people who had a stake in the library because they had made their investment "toward promoting education, happiness, and prosperity in our village."

As it turned out, friends of one proposition traded votes with friends of the other. "Might as well vote for both as for one," as a villager commented laconically. In the final vote at the April 23, 1926, election the library was approved by a very large vote, 587 to 304. The band was also endorsed.

What this meant was that in the spring of 1927, a year later, taxes would be collected to underwrite a community library to the amount of one thousand dollars. Also in the spring of 1927 a village library board would be elected. Meanwhile, the community library association would conduct the library until they turned over all library property to the new board to be elected the following April.

With an energetic and dedicated board, the library, free to all, where any registered card-holder could take out as many as five books, made a good start. Those who had made pledges during the recent drives were reminded that Arthur McElhose was waiting at the Peoples Bank for their needed contributions.

By May, one hundred borrowers had taken out an average of five books. Pledges were coming in so the library could begin to buy new adult fiction with the help of the Illinois secretary of the state's library extension board, which was advising on methods of running the library and the selection of books. The assistant state librarian, Margaret Earle, was helping with the cataloging according to the Dewey Decimal classification. Already the library was a meeting place. There was never enough room at the tables in the crowded facility. More tables were needed. More bookshelves. More desks. More books.

By fall the three hundred registered book borrowers were carrying away two hundred and fifty books every week, almost one a person.

By October the *Herald* was claiming that "all the world's best literature is to be found in the library." High school teachers were urging their scholars to use this excellent new resource. Thanks to careful selection by the book committee, there were "no questionable titles on the shelf."

What really showed the intelligent and careful book selection was the switchover that month. For the first time since Miss Effie and Miss Lucy had invited booklovers into their little living room on North Dunton, there were more adult readers than children readers.

The library was coming of age.

Of course there was still a library functioning in the North School sponsored by the woman's club. Members continued to donate books. The women were a little irked. They "who have continuously worked to build up and keep open a library for the public" felt somewhat snubbed by an idea circulating in town that there had not been a library or "an incentive or opportunity to read" until April 17, 1926. They knew different.

They wanted the public to know that Arlington Heights had a reputation for being a literary town. "In the older days club members from all over the state, and even literary characters, and politicians, statesmen if you please, so referred to it."

It wasn't that the women of the club did not rejoice in the new library. They simply wanted newcomers to know that the Arlington Heights library had an honorable history and sponsors who had worked long without honor—and without remuneration. Once they were assured that the new community library was settled in, the women promised, they would be happy to support it, always with the proviso that recognition be given to their contribution.

Meanwhile, the library couldn't keep up with the demand for the newest books. The Tri-Sigmas had come through for the library before. Now the board turned to them to raise the money for the new books the public was clamoring for. The Tri-Sigmas agreed to arrange an old-fashioned box social, with hometown entertainment provided as an added fillip.

The women who brought mysterious goodies tucked under pretty napkins for the auction were admitted free. All others paid a quarter. Before the supper in the library room above the bank, local singers took the stage, William Kopplin showed a number of his pictures of the Southwest, and Gus Framburg performed a monolog.

The library collection grew by thirty-six volumes, including A. A. Milne's *When We Were Very Young* and Beatrix Potter's *A Tailor of Gloucester,* as well as the adult fiction.

The six board members had settled in well during their year together. Readers were pleased at the selection available when they hiked up to the second floor reading room. The librarian was finding the state library extension board responsive in ways that made the librarian herself more helpful to readers. The Tri-Sigmas continued to be interested and cooperative.

Why make changes, the board asked, when the literary way lies smooth? Why don't we simply run for the board seats we already have and maintain our service? They could see that the sensible course was to draw lots for staggered terms. In the end, N. Moore Banta and Adella Guild ran for the one-year terms, Lillian Russell and Arthur McElhose for the two-year terms, and Frank Sachs and John Beaty for the three-year terms.

The library slate had no opposition. Even the village races would go down as some of the "cleanest" in history as Mayor P. J. Mors was challenged by blacksmith Julius Flentie in a campaign that proved "political propaganda does not necessarily have to have a stench connected with it."

On April 19, 1927, the library association board was elected to serve as the community library board. The village of Arlington Heights had now taken responsibility for the village library. It was no longer a project of the Arlington Heights Woman's Club or the Tri-Sigma group. The library now had a claim on every citizen, and every citizen had a claim on the library.

At the first regular meeting of the legally elected board, Banta nominated John Beaty, who was elected president. Sachs was elected secretary and McElhose treasurer. All the property and holdings of the Arlington Heights Community Library were now turned over to the Arlington Heights Public Library.

Frances Jenkinson was retained as librarian two days a week at $2.50 a day. The room above the Peoples Bank continued to be rented at $16 a month.

As a strategy for keeping the collection up-to-date, the board decided to initiate a rental shelf for new titles. Patrons would pay two cents a day to rent a bestseller that otherwise might not be available.

Satisfied with their year of operation the public library board pretty much retained the status quo. But over at North School the women in the club were assessing the situation of their library. Throughout the winter of 1926-27 they'd stuck to their post, lending out seventy-five books a week to the clients who perused their shelves, mainly the school children. Nellie Best had continued to add books to the collection, as she had done for so many years.

Close as she was to the operation, Mrs. Best could see the time had come to accept the inevitable. At the April 6 meeting, just prior to the April 19 election, she moved that the women in the club donate their books to the new public library at the annual meeting.

The women were generous enough to "hail with joy" the acquisition of "a place to house a public library and keep open a reading room." Nonetheless, before they took their final vote dissolving their library on April 20, the day after the election, the women of the club wanted to say once more, for the benefit of newcomers, that Arlington Heights had had a library for at least eighteen years, "only because of the

Nellie Noyes Best

64

women's impelling desire to benefit the children and the book lovers of the town."

The women recognized that their library was being squeezed into more and more inconvenient space as more children attended North School. They pointed out that their goal had always been a public library paid for by public taxes and "furnished with a suitable reading room."

At their April 20 meeting, president Adella Guild reported on a League of Women Voters talk she'd heard on six keys to success: humor, tolerance, courtesy, diagnosis, consultation, and consideration. The women in the club needed all these, and more, to gracefully vote their library out of operation that day. Since 1887 they had identified themselves in their own minds with the library project, seeing themselves as the preeminent bearers of culture to their village.

However unselfish their interest in the public welfare, the women couldn't totally repress distressing twinges of vexation that they had been passed over, that their contribution was accepted but not sufficiently applauded. They were in the straits of Effie Shepard when she petitioned for a paid position in the North School library. She was passed over with a note of thanks.

Adella Guild, as president, was the official donor of the women's eleven hundred, or fourteen hundred, or sixteen hundred—depending on the source—books at the first regular meeting of the legally elected library board. Like Effie, the women got a vote of thanks.

It was a markedly anti-climatic ending for the enterprise which had been undertaken with such promise and joy. But it didn't end the affinity between the women of the club and the library of their dreams. They would always be available when they were called upon. They knew that and so did the library board.

8.
The Merger

"We couldn't afford ice," an old-timer thinks back, her attention on the days when spending ten cents for a movie ticket was out of the question. "We couldn't afford ice cream, or train fare to Chicago. We couldn't afford anything."

Yet her husband was one of the fortunate wage earners with a job, making fifteen dollars a week working for the village. Even with that security he had to scrounge to feed his family. Every day after work he washed bottles at the local dairy to get free milk for his children. "Without ice we couldn't keep milk from one day to the next. We had to drink it when we got it. It didn't taste that good, warm, but it was healthy for the kids and we were grateful to have it."

Like a lot of other families in Arlington Heights during the Depression, this family lived with relatives. "We had to give up our house and move in with my sister and her family. She had three kids, so did we. Then my brother had to move in. Eleven of us in that little house. We helped each other. It's a good thing we had a garden.

"We lived off that garden. We canned everything. Beans. Cherries. Rhubarb. Pumpkins. Peaches. Tomatoes."

Both banks in Arlington Heights failed during the Depression, taking the nest eggs of many families with them. Developers lost property because they couldn't pay assessments. Owners closed down their businesses because their capital had evaporated.

Stray hired hands worked for their board on nearby farms,

glad to eat. Others came around to peoples' back doors asking for leftovers, a cup of coffee, a dime for a piece of pie.

The dimes didn't always go for food. To this day folks remember handing out money for food and watching the recipient duck into the closest tavern.

The village itself was in the red. School District 214 paid its water bill in surplus chairs. Schools needed the water; the village could use the furniture. Teachers' salaries were cut and, even so, there was no cash to pay them. Teachers received warrants with a promise to pay once tax money was again available.

Villagers struggled to take care of each other. Churches and social groups combined to handle emergency cases. Farmers brought their produce into a canning kitchen on north Evergreen opposite the theater. The first day 130 cans were filled by nine volunteer women. Another group served hot meals at lunch to women and children at the Vail-Davis building. Twelve thousand meals were served in eight months.

Unemployed men signed on with the Civil Works Administration and carried out public works projects, clearing the Salt Creek basin and the Des Plaines River, painting fire hydrants, putting in playgrounds and skating ponds.

Construction of the swimming pool and field house at Recreation Park excited the children who had pretty much relied on themselves to create entertainment. That was late in the thirties. The men hired by the WPA (Works Progress Administration) built athletic fields, improved roads, and built the town's first swimming pool.

That is, the town's first formal swimming pool. There had always been ponds and swimming holes where boys gathered in summer. During the Depression kids preempted the shells of half-finished houses as playgrounds. Stephen Urick recalls a flooded basement in Sherwood which he and his friends regularly used as a swimming pool. John Annen played basketball in an abandoned—for the time—home in Scarsdale with a cathedral ceiling. "I often go by and think of the fun we had there. It's a beautiful house today."

In the thirties those homes were empty because no one could afford to finish them. Handsome houses in subdivisions were planned for the rich. Now most everyone was poor. Even the new library, which had been planned to run on a shoestring, was poor.

Like all the village departments, the library was not getting tax money to pay its debts. Because there wasn't much chance of collecting any taxes for six months, the library board borrowed a total of six hundred dollars from one of its members in 1929 and 1930 to cover fixed expenses. On September 21, 1929, the board canceled Sunday library hours. There was no money to pay the librarian for three hours of work. A dollar and a half.

With no way of knowing that there was a cash crunch ahead, the village board had made plans in the twenties for an expanded village hall. The one-story village hall/fire station in the triangle at Davis and Vail had solid ancestry. The municipal building it replaced had been part of Dr. Frederick Miner's store, a building on Arlington Heights Road whose history went back to days before the railroad came through.

That early building was moved from the site in the usual "musical buildings" fashion of Arlington Heights which made it seem that almost every building had once stood somewhere else. A brick replacement was constructed in 1913. As hard times encroached on village expectations, the village fathers were in the process of expanding that minimum structure into a neatly dentillated two-story flat-iron building, taking advantage of the triangle location as the bank had at Davis and Evergreen.

Municipal building, library site, 1930-1952

To show how solidly the new library had been consolidated into the village system, the board planned a permanent home for the library as well as offices for infant welfare and community nurse workers on the second floor. The council chamber, the business office of the village, and the police headquarters occupied the first floor. The older building to the west housed three pump rooms, the jail (the finest northwest of Chicago), quarters for the fire and police departments, and a tool room and workship for the street and water departments.

The library was now officially blessed by the village with its own tax base, its elected board and its quarters under the cupola of the new town hall. Velda Utterback who succeeded Frances Jenkinson as librarian praised the new situation, its delightful setting and "the light, airy restful room harmoniously decorated and pleasingly lighted."

The books were carted to their new quarters in wooden troughs, similar to small pig troughs. It took Fred Winkelman and George Hughes two days, from February 24 to 26, 1930, to tuck the books into their troughs, heave them into village trucks and trundle them up the long flight of stairs into the library's new home on the second floor. The staff was equally efficient. They were checking out books that Wednesday afternoon, the 26th, to curious borrowers who came to inspect the library's sunny accommodations.

The Arlington Heights Woman's Club, forever a friend in need to the library, had collected more than eighteen hundred dollars over the years for a library fund. Raids on that stockpile had been plotted from time to time, but tenacious library fans had routed any possibility of inroad. The fund was still intact.

When the first negotiations were made for a library over the Peoples State Bank, members of the woman's club tried to soften floating rumors that they opposed the movement. While they realized that they themselves had not been successful in getting a library tax passed, still a real library paid for by public funds had always been their aim. And continued to be. "Should a sufficient fund be thus raised, no group of citizens will be more pleased at the possibility of a public library than the Woman's Club."

The women had pointed out that no one would be happier to cooperate than they when the funds were in sight to establish a permanent public library for the whole public, and a suitable place provided, with a board elected by the public.

The women were as good as their word. When the library was established above the Peoples State Bank, they'd donated their entire collection from the North School.

Now that the library was moving from the bank to the village hall, Nellie Best moved that the woman's club library fund be used to buy suitable furnishings for a library room in the new addition. The motion to spend the eighteen hundred dollars laboriously collected against this very eventuality was passed on February 20, 1929, at a rising unanimous vote.

The club president appointed Mrs. Cyrus Draper, Mrs. Charles Fitzpatrick, and Mrs. Fred Lorenzen, with Mrs. Best as chairman, to serve as the purchasing committee. They worked with the superintendent of library extension in Springfield, Miss Anna May Price, to select the furniture.

There was a delay between the time that the furniture was ordered and the library room ready for it because the contractor for the building died. The furniture actually purchased in 1929 was held in Chicago, then, until the building was finished. The funds bought the furniture, bronze plates identifying the donor as the Arlington Heights Woman's Club, window shades, a clock, a magazine rack, and one touch of romance—a picture of Sir Galahad.

It was February 17, 1930, before the women made their actual presentation. The current president, Eleanor Hausam, asked Nellie Best to detail for the board the woman's club role in the development of the library. Mrs. Best, long identified as the spirit of the North School library, described its beginnings at the Shepards, its move to the public school, the book collecting, and the establishment of the library fund which they were now in the process of spending.

Our idea, Mrs. Best said, was to build a small library building. "However, changing conditions made this impractical and unnecessary." She credited the strong vote for the library tax to the work of the women in showing the children, who were now grown-up voters, how desirable a library was in a community.

71

Mayor Peter Mors accepted the gift of the woman's club on behalf of the village and the people. John Beaty, chairman of the library board, expressed the board's appreciation, stating that the public library of Arlington Heights was now said to be the best equipped of any this side of Chicago.

The women were reasonably nettled when they lost their front position as purveyors of culture to the village. Yet they reacted graciously. They were rewarded for their generous impulse not only with the gratitude of the village, but also with the knowledge that they had spent their money in the nick of time.

The Arlington Heights Bank closed with the balance of their fund in their account. But they had only $34.20. They collected $10.26 of that sum later. Had they hung on to the $1989.30 which they spent for new library furniture, their loss would have been very painful.

9.
Only Uplifting Books

In oral histories taken in the 1980s from Arlington Heights residents who remembered the early days of the century, villager after villager acknowledged his or her hankering for the days when Arlington Heights was truly the City of Good Neighbors, "when everyone knew everyone else."

"It was a different time," a villager will say. "People helped people. Everybody was invited to everything. If you had any work around your house, people would come and pitch in."

Marjorie Annen Carter recalls Dr. Elfeld, one of the town's beloved doctors. Plagued with sties as a child, Carter would sometimes wake with her eyes stuck shut from drainage. Her mother would bathe them open with boric acid solution and send her off to Dr. Elfeld, his fee of fifty cents in hand. Attended by her sister, Carter would ring his doorbell on her way to school. He would carefully lance her sty. When Carter handed over the fifty cents with her right hand, he would press it back into her left, "It hurt me more than it hurt you."

Stephen Csanadi described banking in the days of good neighbors as very social and trusting. "My father would send me up to Mr. Redeker at the bank for money. I was ten or twelve. Mr. Redeker would ask me how much my father wanted, count it up, put it in an envelope and send me home. If you were honest, you were honest. All you had to be was honest."

Henry Leark found that same trust in the lumberyard owner. Leark needed building materials. Married eleven months, working part-time at Benjamin Electric, he bought a lot from his father. Once he had shown his tax bill to the lumber dealers where Hill-Behan is now, they gave him everything necessary to construct a three-room house. "Sand and gravel for the foundation," Leark recalls. "Cement, sewer tiles, all the lumber I needed, and nothing down."

It took Leark three years to pay the lumberyard for the materials. No collateral. No interest. "They were glad to get the business," Leark says. "If I had five or ten dollars, I'd bring it in to them. Folks trusted people more in those days. I'd say that the materials for my three rooms cost between two and three thousand dollars."

Everyone liked the idea of walking uptown and having a nodding acquaintance with the drugstore owner and the grocer and the blacksmith. Indeed, with everyone on the street.

That intimacy also included control, for if everyone knew you everybody knew what you were doing. And everyone had an idea about what you should be doing.

This included a notion about what a person should be reading. From the start the selection of books for the library was an issue. It wasn't only Nellie Best who thought she knew what was good for everyone—and what was suitable reading material for them.

The library committee of the woman's club had always exercised careful judgment when they spent their accumulated quarters. "We did not put on the shelves of our library the works of authors not worthy of a place in the best literature, and we did not put in the hands of children books containing characters unfit for them to associate with in real life."

There was an atmosphere of uplift. The Observer column in the *Herald* in the twenties harked back to Emily Draper and her library days, reminding readers how strongly Mrs. Draper had advocated biographies of good men and women as "an incentive to young readers" to lead exemplary lives themselves. "Lives of great men all remind us, we can make our lives sublime."

During the time that the Tri-Sigmas were stumping for a community library they consistently stressed the necessary care a library should take in the selection of books. "The present so-called modern literature requires most careful censoring."

It wasn't only "modern" books that were suspect. The Tri-Sigmas suggested that because religious matters should be kept out of library work, "let's even be careful about what religious books are placed in the library."

The Tri-Sigma columnist noted that in a nearby town a book was offered to the library by the pastor of a different church. "The book referred to his denomination only. It was not accepted. Later another pastor offered a book representing his denomination and it was not accepted. Some books are about religion in general and these are good for a community to read, but when denominations may appear to endeavor to promote their own work, at the expense of other denominations, that is not a work that can rightfully be included in a public library."

In his own church John Beaty, the Tri-Sigma sponsor, promoted the most elevating examples of literature. He invited young persons to join his discussion class on the books in *The Pocket University,* examples of the writings of American, French, and English writers of prose, poetry, and humor.

Other churches, building up libraries of their own, expressed interest in what books their parishioners might find in the community library. The Reverend Carl M. Noack pointed out that St. Peter's Luthern Church had a good collection of books in its Sunday school or church library. "In selecting books it is always safe to steer shy of best sellers.

Some of them are unfit for anyone to read. Beware of bad books."

That attitude was reflected in the Observer's Notes in the *Herald*. In a May 7, 1926, column the author included a pointed ditty beginning, "Take, O, take these books away."

The anonymous author had little use for popular authors, proscribing "Conrad, Hugh and Zane Grey/Curwood, Sinclair, Fanny Ferber/Welles and Shaw, the great disturber." S/he would also have libraries banish:

> *Sober, thoughtful Philip Gibbs*
> *Irwin Cobb with Funny quips*
> *Sanburg* (sic), *Lindsey and the lot*
> *Stirring up the "melting pot,"*
> *Making all the great mistake—*
> *Things grotesque a poem make.*

And whom would the bard have the villagers read instead of Shaw, the great disturber, and Zane Grey? "Take the seething lot away/Bring us Shakespeare, Burns and Scott/Something solid for today."

The columnist feared that people who had an unhealthy taste acquired through "reading movie tragedies and other exciting tales" would find uplifting books too "slow."

Fortunately, the persons who held the library purse strings were also in favor of uplift. Surely that was true of Nellie Best and her staunch backers. When the library board was elected, villagers chose two men who were authors themselves and editors of publications. Lillian Russell, who was chairperson of the book selection committee for many years, was an experienced teacher, and eminently trustworthy in the eyes of her fellow citizens.

Most everyone in Arlington Heights believed that Lillian Russell and her sister Irene were "two of God's good people." The two sisters were in education all their lives, for their father founded a private school for boys in Highland Park, Illinois, which was later absorbed into Northwestern Military Academy. They grew up in the company of the small boys who were their father's charges, and later taught the next generation of youngsters who came there.

After they had moved into a house kitty-corner from St. John's Church at Evergreen and St. James, the sisters were only steps from North School where they are remembered into the 1980s as beloved. Stephen Urick describes Irene Russell as the "kind of teacher who would hold you on her lap all afternoon if you took a bad tumble on the playground at noon."

Always generous with their time and energy, the Russell sisters had a reputation for beautifying their surroundings wherever they were, a boon for the children growing up in their care.

After their stint at North School, Lillian Russell transferred into the Chicago school system, teaching for many years at the Onahan School in Norwood Park, and Irene went on to serve as principal of the new South School in Arlington Heights, "out on the edge of town." The school looked out on farmland on three sides.

It wasn't only for the children of the town that the Russells expended their energies and care. When the flu epidemic after World War I blighted their village, the sisters staffed an emergency hospital in the unoccupied Methodist parsonage. Even before the Tri-Sigmas began to call attention to the problems of immigrants confused and discouraged by the difficulties of their debut into a new society Lillian Russell was providing them a night school education. When it was augmented under the program the Tri-Sigmas urged, Lillian Russell stayed on, patiently instructing the parents at night just as she did their children by day.

Visitors to the Russell home felt welcome and relaxed under their "exquisite understanding and unselfish devotion."

That same steady vigilance and studious consideration which underlaid the words Lillian Russell spoke to all her students, young and old, she brought to the selection of the written word which was her library board responsibility. With all her other duties, she not only made the selection with the help of her board members, she also filed a continuing column in the local paper describing the books on the shelves so that adults would enjoy their library experience, and parents would find out what new adventures were available to them to "read again, Mommy," to their toddlers.

Lillian Russell and John Beaty were of one mind about this issue of salutory books. He, of course, had expressed his conviction often in the *Herald* columns about the importance of putting the right books into villagers' hands.

What this narrative indicates is the power that local people held over book choice. When the women in the Arlington Heights Woman's Club were filling the shelves, they kept a careful eye on the titles. There was no question that Nellie Best had her standards of restraint and good taste. With the advent of an elected library board the responsibility went to schoolteacher and trusted counselor Lillian Russell, Adella Guild who had served as president of the woman's club, and Frank Sachs, a house painter and decorator who lived in the first floor of John Beaty's home on Euclid. They were in charge.

While local women with more dedication than training were librarians, this condition caused no controversy. But the watershed moment was coming when local women could no longer manage the library. The board would recognize a professional librarian was needed.

Children's books by John Yocum Beaty

The board's first attempt to seek greater qualifications in an accredited librarian would founder on this very basic question of who should select the books.

There was no controversy, however, over the acceptance of one of the new books furnished on August 29, 1930. Board member John Y. Beaty, the Tri-Sigma's teacher, presented the Arlington Heights Library with a copy of his first book, *Billy Berk, The Story of a Berkshire Pig.*

Indirectly, this event presaged the eminence that the library was advancing toward. In 1930 fewer than five thousand villagers lived, most of them, within four or five blocks of the North Western Railroad station with its railroad parks, its grain elevator, and the third track which was completed that year to deal with the increased ridership.

Of those five thousand, six were chosen by the citizenry to sit on the library board. And of those six, as mentioned earlier, two had the talent to be published authors: Banta, head of the temporary Arlington Heights Community Library, and Beaty, the president of the first elected library board. John Beaty's publishing career would continue into the 1940s.

Beaty, of course, was a Methodist, just as the librarian Mary Jane Baxter was. In spite of the Tri-Sigma's declaration that the library should be non-partisan, not dominated by Methodists, natural gravitation pulled Methodists to the library like apples to the grass.

To the Methodists the situation seemed perfectly normal. Beaty had focused on the library in his work with the Tri-Sigmas. When Mary Jane Baxter was librarian over a nineteen-year span, it was the most natural scenario imaginable that she'd mention a vacancy at the library to a woman in her church circle. Most of the women who signed on at the library were looking for a few extra dollars, "something interesting to do a couple of hours a week."

Typically, a person hired to shelve books for a day and a half a week would move up to the check-out desk and, having learned the simple routines necessary for a one-room library that lent out sixty-five books a day, would be available when the informal process of choosing a librarian began.

It is certainly true that the Tri-Sigmas boosted Presbyterian N. Moore Banta as president of the first library board because of his excellent qualifications. It is also true that they declared that "if Jesus were here to select this library board, we believe that he would select without regard to denomination or creed, and we hope the people will make the selection in the same way."

It's in the record that it was Banta himself who nominated John Beaty as president of the first elected library board.

Nonetheless, what looked innocent to the Methodists looked collusive to some library-users. They saw the library as a "closed group." As an observer remembers, "It seemed funny at the time. If you were a Methodist you got in as librarian, or you got a job there.

"That's just how it was."

10.
Surviving The Depression

Waiting for a toddler to mount, riser after riser, to the high second floor of the municipal building goaded some parents to a natural impatience at the inconvenience of the town library. That staircase was also a trial to older people whose knees had grown a little stiff.

Upon arrival in the book-lined chamber above the fire station any annoyance was dissolved in the warmth of the welcome from the staff. If Arlington Heights was the City of Good Neighbors, the library was the epitome of neighborly concern. Once it was Effie Shepard who read to little children in her living room. On the second floor of the municipal building the tradition persisted. Staff members took a genuine interest in patrons' preferences.

"They were always so wonderfully friendly," a long-time-ago reader recalls. "After a couple of visits they knew us and called us by name. And they had found out what kind of book interested us.

"I remember that when I walked in, a librarian would say, 'We have a new book you are going to like. Do you want us to put you on the list for it?' Or 'We're getting that novel you asked about.'

"The service was intensely personal."

Newcomers from other small towns in the Midwest felt at home because the library reminded them of the library at home in Bushnell, Illinois, or Muscatine, Iowa.

During the Depression there were not that many new

Library room, municipal building

books. But the friendly atmosphere did not shatter with the Wall Street crash. The staff continued to do what it could with what it had.

Velda Utterback was the librarian when the library moved into the municipal building quarters in February, 1930. The library had 3,572 volumes including all the Tri-Sigmas had collected and the donations from the Arlington Heights Woman's Club. In the ten hours the library was open each week—2 to 5 p.m. and 7 to 9 p.m. on Wednesdays and Thursdays—staff checked out three hundred books.

Within a couple of months of the opening of the new municipal building library, Velda Utterback was pregnant.

Her mother, Mary Jane Baxter, who was lonely in a new town, offered to take over temporarily.

A cordial, homey woman, Baxter flowered behind the check-out desk. "She wasn't much of a business woman and she had no librarian training," a colleague recalls, "but she was smart and a good all-round person."

Although she was the busy mother of eight children, Baxter read all the new books. "She often said," her daughter remembers, "that she would never give a book to a young person without knowing the contents. She made friends with the kids, and I still meet people who say my mother chose their books for them and helped them start a life of reading." Her daughter recalls helping out at the library (even though she had a job in the Chicago Loop) "because mother didn't ask for many salaried people as she wanted the money for new books."

What penetrated the village consciousness was Mary Jane Baxter's warmth and charm. To many patrons she was the soul of the library.

The second floor over the municipal offices wasn't the best of all possible book worlds, in spite of Baxter's efforts. While everyone applauded the Mom's apple pie atmosphere, not everyone who moved to town came from the boondocks. One new patron who made the demanding trek up the city hall stairs didn't find amenities she was used to. "I didn't expect books stored in orange crates, most of them tattered and torn anyway." As a newcomer, she had no way of knowing how hard-pressed the library was for funds, to a point where there was no money for rebinding.

This was the depth of the Depression. The library had borrowed money from Moore Banta to pay the essential salaries. The board struggled to cut any possible expense. After the directors cut Sunday afternoon hours to save $1.50

a week, they found that they couldn't afford the tab for their Wednesday and Thursday hours either. Would Mrs. Baxter be willing to serve as librarian for the fines and the rental fees on the few new books they owned, the board wondered?

Even as they made their offer, the board members were aware that they didn't plan to buy any more rental books and that rental fees were dropping off. Loyal to the core, Mrs. Baxter agreed to the terms although she realized that things were getting so grim that most patrons didn't have the two cents a night necessary to tuck P. G. Wodehouse's *Big Money* or Zane Grey's *Arizona Ames* into their shopping baskets for a good evening's read.

Fortunately, Mrs. Baxter's loyalty was matched by others. Members of the Arlington Heights Woman's Club recognized how serious were the library's straits and sponsored two card parties to improve the stock. The booty was twenty-one books, fodder for the rental shelf. On a continuing basis, villagers—at this time, George Dunton, Ann Nichols, Mrs. Max Martz, and the Hubert Smiths—culled their personal collections for library donations.

Mary Jane Baxter

84

About this same time, in the early months of 1931, the first breach was created in the library board which had served the village since 1926. John Beaty moved his family out of his comfortable home on Euclid and could no longer chair the board. Bruce Jarvis was nominated to fill out his term and Moore Banta was elected to the presidency, resuming the position he had first accepted in 1926. Before the year was out Moore Banta died suddenly of myocarditis after an illness of less than a day. His death was a terrible shock to his family, to his friends, and to his community. Banta's only daughter, Elizabeth Mueller, was traveling with her husband in South America when her father died. She rushed back. Banta had served as trustee and ruling elder for the First Presbyterian Church. "A leader in almost every activity of a community nature," and an influence "of special force behind various movements for community welfare," as the *Herald* characterized him, Banta was a member of the high school board and the park board as well as the library board. Clarence I. Davis was nominated to fill the vacancy left by Moore Banta and placed on the ballot. An era had ended.

The original library board with its authors and its teachers and its bank cashier embraced the torch passed on by the woman's club and the Tri-Sigmas. They'd looked at the thousand dollars and the thousand books collected by the Tri-Sigmas and envisioned a library which would be "everyman's university," a place where every person in Arlington Heights could get an education, the experience of reading of lives different from their own, the pleasure of prose and poetry. Patrons had only to walk to Vail and Davis and climb that celebrated flight to the second floor.

The board's vision threatened to founder on the shoals of the Depression, but the board did not lose faith. Moore Banta personally lent the library the money to keep its doors open. Board members made do with donated books, shorter hours, and hope for the future.

New board members came on in discouraging times. The local Paddock paper editorialized about the bravery of citizens who were willing to run for public office when there was so little they could offer the public. "Nearly all municipalities are having financial troubles and many aldermen are gladly retiring, but there are new fellows in many places who are anxious and willing to assume the responsibility of taking over the troublesome jobs as village officials."

The officials who were elected would not have to worry about improvements in their villages. There was no money for them. They wouldn't accuse their opponents of misdeeds. There was nothing to finance them. "There is little that can be promised as regards the future," the paper noted, because there were no funds to dip into for rosy-promise projects.

"With empty treasuries," the writer continued, there was little the present officials could do more "than keep the street lights turned on and pay the labor bills."

Yet there were villagers willing to take on the responsibilities of board work and wrestle with the difficulty of deciding whether they could spend any of their hard-come-by dollars on rental books or on rebinding the tattered covers of the most popular volumes. While there was always a full slate ready to run in the library election, there was never any opposition.

By 1933 the Arlington Heights Public Library was receiving a share of the 1931 taxes and could pay off the money it owed the Bantas. Gradually, there were going to be improvements.

Having the library space provided by the village was a tremendous boon for the library. In 1934 further largesse included cleaning and decorating. Because of technicalities arising out of the death of the contractor and lack of funds, the municipal building had not been finished when it was opened in 1931. Just as the WPA built the Recreation Park fieldhouse in the depths of the Depression to the benefit of the men who poured the concrete and sawed the lumber, and of the generations of children who would use the facilities, so the municipal building profited from the Civil Works Administration. Through this program workers were hired to clean and finish decorating the home of the village government, the police department, the fire department—and the library. What with new accessions, many donated, that spic-and-span, "as neat as any home," library now shelved 6,000 volumes. The total circulation for the last quarter of 1933 was 11,298 books. There were one hundred new registrants.

There were over twenty rooms in the municipal building. Civil Works Administration hirees used 250 gallons of paint, mostly various shades of tan, on the building. Many outsiders, according to the paper, termed it the "finest structure of its kind northwest of Chicago."

No one complained about the noise. The patrons were happy to have a library. Nonetheless they noticed when the "huge monster" of a fire truck with its dual-wheel chassis of thirty-eight feet, its eighty-gallon water tank, its thousand feet of fire hose, 240 feet of ladder equipment, its water tanks with force pumps, its revolving fire nozzles, its respiratory equipment—and its sirens—rumbled out of the fire station below where it was regularly stabled. The clangor shook the library's hush.

Fire engine forays were unscheduled, but infrequent. The chug-chug of the steam engine on the North Western tracks easily visible from the municipal building was an established interruption as daily trains served clients at the line's busiest station. Librarians and patrons were grateful for their retreat, but they could hardly call it restful.

The library didn't take any giant steps during the thirties and the war years. It took baby steps. After the taxes started coming in during 1933, conditions improved incrementally. Not only was Mrs. Banta paid back, Mrs. Baxter's salary was reinstated—after all, fines and rentals came to only $110 annually.

The board members rounded up the books that needed cosmetic surgery at the bindery. With the new library tax law, the money due the library from taxes was paid directly by the County Treasurer. Because both banks in Arlington Heights had closed by this time, Arthur McElhose opened a library account at the Mount Prospect Bank.

By 1935 the library could be kept open from 3 to 9 p.m., right through the supper hour which was a great convenience for patrons, on Monday, Wednesday, Thursday, and Saturday. The Boy Scouts took up collecting, making a door-to-door canvas for used books as one of their good deeds. There were funds for rental books which were bought sometimes by the board president, other times by book selection chairman Alfred F. Capps.

At one point the impoverished village board asked the library board to pay their own lighting and heating bills. They retracted their request when they realized how poor the library really was. Board president Clarence Davis explained that the library's tax rate was limited by law and that it was only with the greatest economy that the library was able to function—without the additional worry of paying for the light and heat.

Enough new books were purchased that the library had to install a new stack capable of holding 750 books. Evidently the state, like the village board, was prodded into action by libraries' distressing circumstances. The Arlington Heights

Public Library received a "relief check" for $250 from Springfield.

That was real largesse. The library could afford an up-to-date *Webster's Dictionary* and the new *Columbia Encyclopedia*. Girls got the *American Girl*. Boys got *Open Road for Boys*. Adult readers got *Time* and *Aviation*. About this time the library was solvent enough to buy books seventh and eighth grade teachers requested to supplement their students' texts.

In 1937 when the library was open from 3 to 9 p.m. every weekday except Thursday, the library purchased *Compton's Encyclopedia*. That year three hundred books were lent to North and South Schools. Again the teachers were able to select what they needed.

A telephone was installed for a six-month trial in 1939. That year the library could swing the expenses of an additional day a week. Through the years up to and including the first years of World War II, library finances steadily improved. The librarian's salary went up to eighty dollars a month in 1941 and one hundred dollars a month in 1942. The school extension service improved. It was made available to students at St. Peter's Lutheran and St. James Catholic schools.

Considerable changes were in the offing for the library as the war came to an end, but villagers would remember their bantam—"it was really very small"—library in the municipal building with great fondness. They would think back on Velda Utterback and her lovely contralto voice—"the sweetest person"—and her mother Mary Jane Baxter—"she dreamed of a new library building." Ione Lawbaugh—"a true lady, quiet and reserved"—and Dorothy Mitchell, a capable woman, served for short terms before Florence Kule took over.

The library wasn't a gathering place. There simply wasn't room. But it was a source of gratification for many patrons. Perhaps one person's story can stand for all, can show what the Arlington Heights Public Library meant in the lives of the villagers.

The library encouraged vacationers to take books along on their trips. Four books could be checked out for as many as four weeks. One young matron in town took novel advantage of the travel offer. She wasn't going anywhere. Her husband was out of work, like many of his neighbors. The couple was low in funds but they didn't lack, as Kenneth Grahame insists many grown-ups do, "the higher gift of imagination."

Her husband would maintain the ramparts of home and hearth, as he'd agreed to do, so she could "sail and sail/with unshut eye/around the world forever and aye" on a barque of books.

"I'm going to have two free weeks and I'm getting away," the young mother told Mrs. Baxter as she checked out her four-book stock of travel-in-Europe books. "My husband is going to do all the housework and look after the children. And I, what am I going to do? How am I going to get away? I'm going to read and read and read."

When this imaginative vagabond swept down the town hall stairs, turned west past the arched fire engine exit and the pretty band shell, thinking of the tickets to wonder she held in her arms, she stood—or skipped, for such was her joy—for all the delight born in that inadequate but beloved book house on Vail and Wing.

11.
A Suitable Memorial

It was 1944. Workers and machines that had been idle during the Depression were now piling up war materiel. The great industrial economy that had stumbled during the thirties was racing to produce. People who had once queued up for soup and taken shelter in municipal lodging houses were working the early shift and taking home bigger paychecks than they had ever collected.

The United States was at war and Arlington Heights shared the action. Boys who had swung from the tough vines in the Douglas Avenue woods and learned the back dive at Recreation Park pool were now far from home. They were part of the Army and Air Force which organized a massive offensive against Germany. They were part of the Navy that won stunning victories at sea. They were part of the Marines who fought in the South Pacific. They were part of the greatest armada ever assembled to go ashore at D-Day on the Normany coast to liberate the European continent.

The people in Arlington Heights were proud of their servicemen and women. Even before the war was over villagers were meeting in committee to decide how they would honor the bravery and enterprise of young graduates of Arlington schools who were risking their lives. Even more poignant was the villagers' impulse to dignify the memory of the young men who would never return.

At that time representatives of all the civic organizations in the town had organized a Community Council. During the winter of 1943-44 members gathered to plan what they hoped was going to be the "greatest celebration in the history of the community." There were delegates from twenty-five organizations at that general meeting called to plan a July 4 observance which would outpoint any ever held in the village.

The July 4 gala was traditionally a big money-maker. Funds collected in 1944 were already earmarked for recreation projects—summertime activities in the park—and a war memorial for those brave men living and dead who had once played on Arlington streets and studied in Arlington schools.

The Community Council had donated fifteen hundred dollars from its 1942 festival for the war memorial. Now the July 4th celebration planned for 1944 was going to make more money than its most sanguine promoters had dared to hope for. In 1942 the summer festival receipts were $2950; in 1943, $3547. In 1944 receipts were going to be over $6,000, and the war memorial fund was going to burgeon by at least $2,000.

Enthusiastic promoters looked at all that money and realized the time had come to make some decision about how the village would honor its service people. Two committees were chosen. Trustees appointed to oversee the fund were Dr. B. T. Best, Arthur H. Franzen, Fred W. Gieseke, Albert E. Goldthwaite, Walter Krause, Jr., Ernest H. Malzahn, William A. Miles, Henry Muller, and Hugo Thal.

The decision to choose what actual form the memorial would take was put in the hands of a committee chaired by J. D. Flentie. Nicholas Lattof, owner of the local Chevrolet agency and a benefactor of the village, who was serving as president of the Community Council at that time, appointed committee members Oral R. Cline, C. E. McWharter, the

Reverend George Stier of St. James Church, Otto Wulbecker, Dr. Edwin W. Baumann, Nat T. Burfeind, Paul Carroll, and Ward W. Teutsch to serve with Flentie. Later, Forest Davis, J. E. Millay, and Fred Gieseke filled vacancies.

When they talked it over, the committee members agreed it would be appropriate to let those who were to be honored by the memorial have some say on what it should be. That would be the servicemen and women and, by extension, the thirty-two Gold Star Mothers in the town. Very soon, however, scores of villagers were citing their preferences.

There was some controversy. A local doctor spoke out strongly for a community hospital. There was no first grade hospital on the Northwest highway between Chicago and Woodstock, he pointed out, stressing how appropriate a memorial hospital would be for those who had suffered and died. He made his proposal to the Lions Club, one of the organizations in the Community Council, one evening after the Lions had satisfied themselves "with generous portions of fried chicken and all of the fixings, served by the ladies of the Lutheran church."

In Dr. H. H. Carr's opinion the hospital would support itself with proper management and "would be able to conduct a certain amount of charity work." The Lions took the suggestion under consideration.

The following year the finance committee of the Independence Day celebration reported a gross income of $9,900.30, of which the War Memorial Fund received $2046.42.

The public had a reserve of dreams which surfaced when the *Arlington Heights Herald* asked readers for New Year's wishes for the community at the beginning of 1946. Not only were there those who favored the development of a fully accredited hospital, there were votes for the metamorphosis of weed patches into playgrounds, adequate housing for citizens, the abolition of all "old and unsightly structures in the village," taverns replaced by a youth center, a tea room "more attractive and serving better food than any other to be found in the Northwest suburban area," a high class antique shop, a modern railway depot, a new post office building— and a public library building.

Oral Cline, then president of the Lions Club and a member of the War Memorial committee, was the second person to make a strong plea for a hospital, a Class A hospital costing in the neighborhood of $250,000. He suggested a five-year financial campaign or pledges over a five year period. There are outside agencies, he said, with funds to help out communities which give evidence that they are willing to spend a lot of their own money to bring a hospital to their town.

The junior vice commander of the Arlington Heights post of the Veterans of Foreign Wars assured the committee that the best possible use of the memorial fund would be a "home and meeting place" for the Veterans of Foreign Wars Post No. 931 of Arlington Heights. The group promised to add funds of its own to enlarge and improve the property on which the post would build. The post also proposed extending the privileges of the building to youth center activities, the Boy Scouts, and the Girl Scouts.

In May of 1946 when the committee was replacing new members and naming Carl M. Teutsch to head a fact-finding committee to survey the facilities in the community, a Chicago newspaper reported that area veterans preferred "useful memorials," including playgrounds, swimming pools, athletic fields, and other projects designed to serve the entire community.

Harry and Vega Freyermuth, Mr. and Mrs. D. K. Scott, and Mr. and Mrs. Arthur Gieseke opted for a memorial gymnasium as a tribute to the boys who went to Arlington

High School. "A number of gold star parents feel that they would like to see this expression manifested in a new gymnasium building for the high school."

Robert Bishop favored dedicating the airfield south of town, constructed by the government, as Arlington Heights Memorial Airport.

John J. Duthorn and William Stirlen of the VFW post wanted lights for the softball field. "Disappointed" asked, "Does anyone really think that lights are an adequate war memorial?"

Ed Wise favored providing one room in a memorial building "to house the historical documents and mementoes of our community." "Watchful" noted when suggestions waned. Was it because of the hot weather?

The *Herald* was responsible for a little editorializing, putting a letter on the front page that recommended a memorial library. The "Arlington Heights official" whose letter was so prominently displayed suggested a number of variations on the bare-bones library so far envisioned. He suggested that plans for a memorial building be selected from the files of leading American architects or by invitation to American architects for "the singular honor plus a nominal fee." He fancied such dramatic features as an ivy-covered clock tower, world map murals or "an illuminated globe with tiny stars marking scenes of Arlington Heights men in action, a band shell and proscenium for open air concerts and programs, and stained glass memorial windows." The window on the west should denote supreme sacrifice; the north, purple hearts; the east, the living, and the south, triumphant victory.

Maintenance for this building, the official contended, could be obtained from the public library tax, administration from the elected library board. The writer used his front page exposure to add that the memorial building should contain

95

and preserve for the future "everybody and everything having some connection with Arlington Heights in the past or present. Pictures of grandpa and grandma, of people with biographies, of old and new buildings, where they were located, their dates and use."

Bill Beckman and Ralph Hauptly were turned off by the library idea. "Books are for old fogies and an extensive library would be a waste of time as far as young people of the town are concerned." They were voting for a town gymnasium.

Having spent several years carefully weighing all the arguments, a brave and confident War Memorial Committee made its recommendation for this important change in village life at their September 9, 1946 meeting.

They recommended that the most suitable war memorial would be a public library built in the Memorial Park bounded by Chestnut, Fremont, and Park Place "dedicated to those who served in the armed forces during World War II and in memory of those who gave their lives."

The committee had done its homework. Members had sounded out the public and considered the public's every suggestion. They had noted the three hundred signatures of persons determined to get night lights at Recreation Park. They'd debated the dedication of a street, the erection of a Scout center, a memorial clinic or hospital, a band shell, a carillon or bell tower, a youth center, and a war memorial shaft.

The committee's proposal was not the last word, even after all their struggle. Villagers still had a chance to jump into the fray when the decision came up at the October 14 Community Council meeting. "Every leading organization is represented on the council," the president said, "yet we want every citizen to share in the selection of a war memorial just as every citizen has shared in the recent war effort."

However, Oral Cline did see fit to point out that a library appeared to meet the requirement of memorializing the sacrifice of servicemen and serving the whole community for the future. And the War Memorial Committee had marshalled solid arguments for a library-memorial:

1) It would serve a useful and public purpose as well as a necessary one.

2) Present library facilities are incompatible with the size of the community.

3) Present library quarters are in demand for the proper administration of village affairs. (The library now occupies a second floor room in the village hall.)

4) Space for books and tables in the present library is inadequate.

5) Architecture and solemnity of such a structure would create a proper background for memorial services by the community and provide an appropriate place for plaques commemorating those who died in service in World War II.

6) The library would serve as a repository for the archives of the community.

7) Because of its community need, the library would have the public appeal requisite for any campaign for funds. Present funds are insufficient.

8) Any memorial will require supervision and financial support after the initial funds have been raised and the project completed. In the case of a library, an existing public body has the know-how to operate it and sufficient income to assure the community of its proper and continued operation.

The committee estimated cost at $50,000. The war

memorial fund was up to seven thousand dollars. Walter Kroeber, chairman of the building committee, was working out a design. A. H. Franzen was chairman of the finance committee. The library would be called the Arlington Heights Memorial Library, its second name change and third name.

Acceptance of the idea of honoring the servicemen of the village with a library was not automatic at the October meeting of the Community Council. Advocates of alternatives still had their say. There was strong support for a hospital until a local doctor argued that many hospitals had gone broke during the Depression and that a neighboring hospital with a base much like Arlington Heights' was continually in the red. The thought of money woes scotched the hospital dream.

The advantage of night lights at Recreation Park was bat-

Fire station under the municipal building library

ted around again, this time linked with a memorial shaft at the park by the American Legion.

On the final vote, members of the Community Council voted for a free-standing municipal library on October 14, 1946. Answering the rollcall that night were representatives of the American Legion, V.F.W., Cub Scouts, Girl Scouts, Lions Club, Methodist Church, St. John's Church, St. Peter's Church, Nurses Club, P.T.A., P.E.O., Park Board, press, public schools, Scarsdale Improvement Association, Woman's Club, Christian Science Church, and the medical profession.

When the Community Council met on November 11, they had to discuss how this library would be funded. Arthur Franzen, the banker, reported on the possibility of building with funds raised by a general village bond issue. Some of the members thought that the council was "taking the easy way out" if they went that route. They advised that a straw poll be taken to find out what the taxpayers wanted. "Would they rather make outright contributions or prefer to have the cost added to their tax bills over a period of years?"

Franzen explained that the library board couldn't authorize the issuance of bonds. What it could do, though, was determine whether or not a building should be erected, where and how long the bonds should run, although they couldn't be over twenty years. The village board would pass the ordinance to issue the bonds. Interest could not exceed five percent.

The committee heaved a large and mutual sigh of relief when they settled the question of the war memorial. Even now there were little burbles of discontent. The ferment that had begun to effervesce when the decision was being made did not settle down after the vote. Townsfolk were still debating. Until they saw an actual building, interested parties considered their input licit.

It had been the same way with the library fund of the woman's club. For years the women pooled their quarters for their consummate dream: a repository for all humanity's wisdom and learning culled into books.

But there were mice who wanted to nibble at the cheese. For one purpose or another, one impatient member or another tried to eat up the fund for other, to them equally satisfying and possibly more immediate, projects. Nellie Best was remembered as the sentinel who safeguarded the stores. In the end the fund was saved for those sturdy pieces of furniture that gave the library over the municipal building all the class it had. Those chairs and tables with bronze plaques reading "Gift of Arlington Heights Woman's Club, January, 1930," were an unbelievable boon to a library trying to operate during a national Depression. Nellie Best and her cohorts were vindicated.

Now the members of the Community Council who had voted for a library as the war memorial had to stand as tall as Nellie Best. Their vote, their official vote favoring the library, took place in October, 1946. As late as May, 1947, a group was touting the notion of a housing project for grade school and high school teachers. In April, 1948, the members of the Lions Club were discussing the old chestnut that had been cracked so many times—lights in Recreation Park as a war memorial.

The representatives of Arlington Heights' civic organizations held to their vote. In December, 1948, librarian Mary Jane Baxter reported to the library board that the American Legion and the Veterans of Foreign Wars had put aside $10,000 to $11,000 as a war memorial fund to be used for a municipal library.

The Arlington Heights Memorial Library was going to become a reality.

12.
The First Bond Issue

"When I hear the words 'inner sanctum,' " Susan Allen Toth wrote in *Blooming,* "I think of the Ames Public Library. It was a massive stone temple, with imposing front steps that spread on either side into two flat ledges, overhung by evergreens." Safely perched on the cool stone blocks, "surrounded by my stacks of new books, I always felt unusually serene, bolstered by the security of the library behind me and the anticipation of the books beside me."

As a student helper in her first library job, Susan Toth returned books to their appointed places. "Although I enjoyed shelving books, finding the infinitesimally exact Dewey decimal numbers between which to sandwich each volume, noting with pride the tidiness of the arrangement when I had finished, I found that within a day all the books were messed up again.

"Other people kept taking them out."

From her earliest days "nested happily in the Children's Room," Susan Toth had always thought of the library as a personal possession, "and I wasn't altogether comfortable about sharing it."

She gave up her idea of being a librarian.

A long roster of Arlington Heights women, like Susan Toth, gravitated to the library because they loved books. They resonated with Joseph Conrad's notion of the artist, the writer, who "speaks to our capacity for delight and wonder, to the sense of mystery surrounding our lives: to our sense of pity, and beauty, and pain."

Although those Arlington women and Susan Toth all began their careers shelving books, their inclinations diverged. The Arlington Heights staff had no massive stone temple, no imposing edifice. They had only the Shepards' living room, the big room over the bank, and, later, the municipal building.

However, the Arlington women who shelved the books in what were never very impressive quarters had the signal virtue of openhandedness which they must have caught, one from another, in a beneficent contagion. For they never seemed sorry when "the books were messed up again" by patrons taking them out. In fact, they were forever putting postcards in the mail to patrons about new purchases which would interest them. "That's what we were there for," Juanita Conrad carefully pointed out when she talked about her years in the library. Arlington Heights women were "comfortable" sharing books.

This pattern obtained over a long period. The thoughts of a woman whose children were all in school would lightly turn to the satisfaction possible in a job that combined part-time employment, sociability and the pleasure of being surrounded by books. She would turn up at the library, asking if there was something she could do.

Mary Jane Baxter was one of these women. Her eight children were well started on their own interesting lives when Mrs. Baxter took over as librarian from her pregnant daughter while the library was still over the bank. She made the library an extension of her own light heart and warm personality. The kind of woman who was known for taking her eight children to Sunday school every Sunday of the year when they were yet at home, Mrs. Baxter "worked constantly to improve the library and make it a valuable asset to the community."

As board member Helen Graham eulogized her, "her pleasant and capable manner, coupled with her genuine interest in all patrons of the library, made a visit a most enjoyable experience. She was especially interested in providing proper reading material for young people, and a whole generation of children acquired their reading habits under her kindly guidance."

During those years when the Community Council was palavering with the villagers about the war memorial, there had been changes in the library at the municipal building. Mrs. Baxter fell ill in 1944 and had major surgery in 1945. To lessen her burden, the board hired Ione Lawbaugh as her assistant at $75 a month, and Edith Lindsey, a retired English teacher who had had a long career at Arlington High School, provided additional services at fifty cents an hour.

By the fall of 1949, Mrs. Laubaugh was appointed acting librarian at $125 a month because Mrs. Baxter's condition was worsening. On October 7, 1949, Mary Jane Baxter who had greeted patrons with the smile of a good book neighbor for nineteen years, died in St. Joseph Hospital in Elgin. She was 72 years old.

The library board, the patrons, the villagers, mourned this benevolent figure who had made them all feel at home in their town library.

Ione Lawbaugh, "a lovely woman" in the pattern of other librarians "lovely and pleasant in their lives," took over Mrs. Baxter's responsibilities. During her short term the library was in a holding pattern. The old order was going to change, but no one knew exactly how to assess the new. When Mrs. Laubaugh announced in the summer of 1951 that she was going to marry Fred Utterback, Mary Jane Baxter's son-in-law, whose wife Velda Utterback had died, some board members wondered whether the time hadn't come to take the facility out of the amateur class into the world of library affairs. Perhaps, now, with a new library on the docket, it was time to hire a professional librarian. Helen Graham who asserted somewhat forcefully that "a library should be more than a morgue for books," was appointed a committee with Blanche Ashton to research the possibility of going professional.

They soon discovered that there were not that many professional librarians available. They interviewed Dorothy Mitchell who had one year of training in library science at the University of Chicago and worked at the library of the Art Institute in Chicago in October, 1951.

As the library saga unfolded, it developed that the library board was not ready for a professional like Dorothy Mitchell, a librarian who wished to choose herself what books would be available in the village library and to exercise some freedom of expression. It wasn't long before board president Paul Patrick was approaching another of the capable and trustworthy (though less adventurous) kind of woman with whom the board was comfortable, to ask her if she would serve as librarian in the new building now going up on Belmont and Miner across from Recreation Park.

Actually, Mr. Patrick had mentioned Florence Kule as a candidate before Mrs. Mitchell was appointed. Now, with some relief and gratitude for her steady strength, Mr. Patrick asked Mrs. Kule if she would serve as librarian.

Until this day Mrs. Kule remembers the evening very well. "I had gone home for my supper and hadn't been back very long when Mr. Patrick beckoned me over to a quiet spot and asked me to be the librarian. I thought, 'What in the world is this?' It seemed to me that the new librarian was going along the way she should."

Mr. Patrick was not very forthcoming. "We've run into a problem and we'd like you to take over for us," he said. Later when Mrs. Kule faced the library board she stressed her lack of experience. But, as she recalls later, "it sounded as if someone had to take hold. That night I told them I would give it a trial run."

She had her doubts about stepping into the position, but the board members "seemed so desperate" to her. She set her apprehensions aside even though she had never done any cataloging or ordering of books. "I couldn't say no to Mr. Patrick. He was so sincere, and the new library was almost complete, ready to move into, and under the circumstances they would be without a librarian."

Florence Kule

105

Paul Patrick was eager to settle the matter with Florence Kule as a woman he felt secure with, someone whom the board could deal with. He had no problem with her lack of specialized education. Mr. Patrick was in full agreement with Aristotle's thesis that "things we have to learn before we can do them, we learn by doing them," even if he couldn't have found the source of the quote. Florence Kule, to Mr. Patrick's mind, was a natural: bright, competent, and willing. He had no doubts about her ability or about her loyalty to the board's expectations or about her aptitude for learning by doing.

Florence Kule had been learning by doing all her life.

She hadn't had the chance at education that her natural abilities warranted because her father, a blind piano-tuner working for The Kimball Company, died about the time that the youngest of his four children was born.

Florence, the oldest, helped her mother by accepting a job at her father's former company when she herself was just fourteen. She continued her high school classes at night. Later she went into secretarial work and skirted the notorious world of Chicago crime by serving for a time as secretary to the father of Nathan Leopold, who was "totally crushed" when his son and his son's friend, Richard Loeb, both brilliant students at the University of Chicago, committed one of the heinous murders of the century as a "perfect crime."

After she married, Florence and her husband slowly peregrinated toward the Northwest suburbs, living briefly in Norwood Park, Edison Park, Prospect Heights, then Mount Prospect where, like her Arlington Heights counterparts with an interest in books, Mrs. Kule found a spot filing and putting books into their "infinitesimally exact spots" on the shelves in the Mount Prospect Library. Interested even then in the mechanics of book selection and processing, Mrs. Kule found herself excluded from the mysteries of that occult knowledge.

She was learning. By the time the Kules moved to Arlington Heights, she was conversant with the basics of library lore and fit easily into a similar position in the Arlington Heights library where she avoided the limelight until Mr. Patrick made his offer. Mrs. Kule's apprenticeship was short.

Not everyone was favorably impressed with the library board's peremptory decision to replace Mrs. Mitchell. A Paddock reporter observed that Mrs. Mitchell had made the library come to life. "In all due respect to past library workers, Mrs. Mitchell is a trained librarian, and consequently could add a professional touch to her job.

"She has revamped the library, purchasing new books, which suited the taste of the majority of patrons, changing the card system, overdue fees, and due dates, making everything as simple as possible for those using library services." Streamlining book check-outs by eliminating library cards and introducing pre-stamped, date-due cards, Mrs. Mitchell got rid of blind files and the possibility of lost and misfiled cards.

Villagers the reporter interviewed voiced similar approval, mentioning that "Mrs. Mitchell went out of her way to select books for patrons, searching the shelves until she found something that would suit the individual's taste."

She took commuters into consideration, buying the pocket editions (paperbound books) which they found "convenient to carry back and forth on the train, thus enabling them to get some reading done in time that otherwise would be wasted."

She worked hard at the cataloging, hiring high school girls to assist. She got free help from woman's club volunteers. She had cautious permission from the board to do book selection, providing she used discretion. Nonetheless by early March Mrs. Graham was suggesting that a committee of board members should be appointed to pass on the selection of books, and by March 28 Mrs. Mitchell was gone. She had been hired at a starting salary of $250 a month on December 1, 1951. She'd hardly had time to ask if she should concentrate on public relations or cataloging before she was displaced with a month's salary in her pocket in the middle of March.

Mrs. Kule was now head librarian at $250 per month.

Board members were grateful for their instant-librarian because they had other concerns. For years the board had wrestled with such weighty decisions as replacements for staff, closing times and rental fees. Should an extra girl get seventy-five cents an hour? Should money be kept in Arlington National Bank?

Overnight, like Jack's beanstalk, their worries grew. Instead of dealing with the problems of a one-room library where the children sat cross-legged to read on a rug brought from home by one of the librarians, the board was looking at sketches of floor plans, debating locations, planning bond issues, and approving contracts.

The final salvo in the discord about the appropriate war memorial was discharged by children writing in an essay contest sponsored by the Lions in connection with their Peanuts Day. Most of the hundred entries suggested that an improved library was the answer to "What Does Arlington Heights Need for Its Children?" Thirty-seven years later, one of the sponsors of the contest remembered that not all youngsters in the village knew about the library. "Library? What library?" some of them asked. Another was scornful. "What library? That half-dozen books?" Acknowledging their influence, Don Hartman said that "when you want the truth, go to the children."

As St. James eighth-grader Geraldine Kuhn succinctly put the thesis common to many of the essays: "A Public Library Tells After All What a Community Is." The community—and the children—were going to get their library. On January 30, 1950, at a special meeting, one of many, the architect Walter Kroeber presented a sketch and floor plan for a yellow-brick and stone building of contemporary design "with a quiet dignified appearance corresponding to the purpose for which the building will be used" to the library board.

Architect Kroeber estimated that the 93-foot-wide and 46-foot-deep building would cost $75,000, not including the lot. The center of the building would be 15 feet high to permit the erection of double stacks in the rear portion. Reading rooms to seat sixty persons would be in wings on each side of the entrance where plaques would be hung honoring the local persons who had served their country.

No site could be chosen nor would the trustees of the War Memorial Fund hand over the money until a bond issue was passed by the voters. At its February meeting the library board passed a resolution to build a new library financed by a bond issue.

March 11, 1950, was the day set for Arlington Heights voters to decide whether bonds in the amount of Eighty Thousand ($80,000) should be issued by the village of Arlington Heights for the purpose of constructing a library building and furnishing and equipping same.

The village board, the library board, and the woman's club worked together. Woman's club members had never lost their zest for promotng the library. This year they had an additional stimulus. The women were entered in a state woman's club contest. Organizing for the bond issue would add many credits to their tally toward winning the five thousand dollar prize for the woman's club which did the most toward bettering its community.

Petitions signed by hundreds of interested citizens had been presented to the village board. Eager supporters organized a telephone campaign to get the facts to the public. The Fence Post in the *Arlington Heights Herald* printed villagers' arguments pro and con. A reader wondered whether the library was really used enough to warrant a new building. "We should not spend this money just to satisfy our pride, simply because another town is building a new library or because our present library is not fancy enough," "Interested Reader" wrote.

The editor answered that over 2500 persons held library cards, that there were 14,500 books on the shelves and little room for more, and that fifty new books were purchased each month. "About one hundred books are taken out each day, half of them juvenile. The library is open six hours five days a week and three hours on Saturday. Every table and chair is occupied after school hours. Is there need to say more?"

In her letter Mrs. Adolf Wiegand was specific about the need for more space. Storage space is non-existent, she wrote. "With a collection of 15,000 books, space affords room for about 10,000." She described every department as squeezed. "The children's reading space is crowded into a twelve-foot by thirty-foot floor area . . . the librarian's working quarters are squeezed into a poorly ventilated corner. . . the stacks are overcrowded and poorly lighted."

Members of the Arlington Heights Woman's Club had conducted a "whirlwind campaign" over one weekend to collect the five hundred signatures necessary to get the village board to call the special election. Now volunteers from that faithful group were spending another weekend burning up the wires and burning in their message in favor of what the *Arlington Heights Herald* called the "much-talked-about, dreamed-about and hoped-for memorial library building."

In order to avoid phone tie-ups, *Herald* readers were prompted to simply say, "I understand the importance of voting Saturday. I will be there," when the volunteer identified herself. Mrs. Charles Heiss, chairperson of the public welfare department of the woman's club, was in charge of the phone campaign to bring out readers' friends.

The women were not the only enthusiasts. The American Legion and the Veterans of Foreign Wars also sponsored passage of the bond issue. At that point in March, 1950, the budget of the library in the municipal building was $6,500 a year, about one-third of the amount that a one mill tax would net. The tax machinery already existed to enable the library board to operate a library building after it was erected.

What was more, villagers were told, it was estimated that the annual budget would require only a small increase in the present tax. The maximum requirement was estimated at less than $10,000.

The *Herald* admitted that it was true that construction was under way on a new library in Mount Prospect. Palatine was negotiating for the purchase of a site obtained from an estate for the low price of $1,700.

There were approximately ten thousand residents in Arlington Heights in the spring of 1950. Thirty-five hundred of them were eligible to vote. Most of them had heard from a zealous woman's club volunteer. Only 580 put voting at the village board room in the village hall at the intersection of Wing and Davis Streets on their list of Saturday morning chores.

Three hundred and fifty-one of those voters put their X next to "Yes." A new library would be built.

William Dean Howells wrote in 1902 that "the man of letters must make up his mind that in the United States the fate of a book lies in the hands of the women." Certainly the fate of the books in the Arlington Heights Public Library lay in the hands of the women of the club. Florence Hendrickson who would serve as president of the Arlington Heights Woman's Club and speak all over the state often made the point, "subject to correction," (but she was never corrected) that eighty-five percent of the libraries in Illinois were begot by women.

If Arlington Heights is any example, then we can see the mechanism. Women collect the books, women find them housing, women find them shelves and rugs and orange crates, women sing their praises, women shelve them in their "infinitesimally exact" places.

And women get out the vote—three hundred and fifty-one votes for the Arlington Heights Memorial Library. Men were interested, men lent their support. But the library was the women's dream—and their creation.

13.
Moving In On Belmont

Nineteen hundred and fifty was the year that "those people" started choking the streets, the schools, the churches of Arlington Heights. "Before 1950," a housewife on north Pine mourned, "we had a lovely old country village to ourselves. That's why we came here. It was so pretty with all the trees. And so clean. Everyone knew each other.

"Then the newcomers came and put houses on all those empty lots where there used to be trees, made us build all those new schools, and took up all the parking spaces.

"Our village lost its old town feeling."

Some said that the owner of one store near Campbell and Dunton, Arlington Heights' "State and Madison," lost his business brooding over his "lost village." He simply couldn't bring himself out of the back of the store when a new customer was in the front. The upheaval was equally painful for many villagers.

Before 1950 corn fields ringed the village. Cherry trees stippled any aerial view. Elms and maples lined the streets except where the sylvan sentinels were felled when Northwest Highway was cut through the town along the railroad tracks.

A movie made in the forties could include every child in the village schools and most of the town's businesses. The village, like the rest of the country, was in a holding pattern over much of that decade because of wartime restrictions on the use of rubber and wood and metals. No houses went up.

113

In the "lovely old country village" where children fit handily into two grammar schools, one north, one south, a one-room library within walking distance of everyone in town could satisfy most browsers' needs.

Suddenly in the fifties, like dandelions sending out their parachutes, builders began to "seed" houses into all the town's cornfields and cherry orchards and pastures where local people drove their cows to graze. "Those people," postwar couples looking for space to raise the big families they had dreamed about during the long years of World War II, robbed the residents of Arlington Heights of their tight little island.

It developed that these new people were readers. They were willing to hike up the stairs to the municipal building library, with their toddlers climbing stolidly behind them. The fledgling readers would choose their own stories and then wait, not always patiently, for their parents to settle on their preferences.

Mary Lee Ewalt, who later was to serve as librarian, recalls her own toddler grabbing a book at random off the stacks and pressing it on her mother to hurry up the selection process. As she put the book back on the shelf next to *The Late George Apley,* Mrs. Ewalt told her little girl, "I don't especially like Marquand."

"My daughter got a completely unwarranted reputation for being erudite," Mrs. Ewalt said later, "when she announced at the check-out desk that her mother didn't especially like Marquand," as if they had been comparing notes on favorite authors.

Now the villagers, that little girl and her mother, and the elderly who, according to the Paddock paper, had expressed a desire to "spend a few quiet hours enjoying our books and magazines" were going to have a new library where their

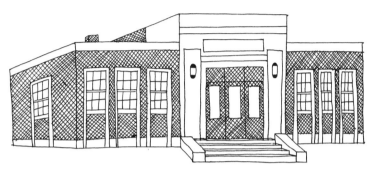

Arlington Heights Memorial Library, 1952-1968

enthusiasm would not be dampened by stairs or orange crates or the constriction of one room.

By October, 1950, construction of a library with three easy stone steps opening onto a two-winged building of "quiet dignified appearance" began at the corner of Belmont and Miner, "as no better sites were offered." Board members, "generally agreed that this was a good location," bought two lots from Emma Kosmin, widow. The two lots on the southwest corner, Lots 1 and 2 of Block 6 of George Dunton's Addition to Arlington Heights No. 2, were of historic interest because they had been part of the original Dunton family holdings.

Architect Walter Kroeber secured bids and let various contracts at a fee of six percent of the cost of the building. The five thousand dollars for Emma Kosmin came out of the eleven-thousand-dollar War Memorial Fund which had been turned over to the library after the referendum on March 11, 1950.

Library board members meeting with representatives of the American Legion agreed that a bronze plaque would be erected on a wall inside the library by the main entrance, a large flag pole would stand on the corner of the lot, and showcases would be installed for display of war souvenirs and documents.

This was really going to be a memorial library, a fitting tribute to the men and women, 437 of them (417 men, sixteen women, one chaplain, and three doctors), who had served in the armed forces during World War II. Forty-one of those who served died on battlefields from Germany to the South Pacific. In dedicating their library, villagers honored those who had risked and lost their lives. The villagers were truly grateful.

Because of continuing war shortages, steel companies could not promise delivery of steel floor joists before January, 1951, so the board approved the use of wood. More than half of the contracts were let to local firms, including cement work to Edwin H. Meyer, painting and decorating to Arlington Home Decorators, electrical wiring and fixtures to Dreyer Electric, plumbing and sewer work to Raymond Wilke.

Not having any notion that the tortoise village of 1950 was going to multiply like a hare in the sixties and the seventies, the library board accepted Walter Kroeber's suggestion that the library should be designed to store 30,000 volumes, a standard library size for a city of 10,000 to 12,000 persons.

Who was predicting in 1950 that Arlington Heights was going to surpass the population of some state capitals? That those 8,768 persons who needed 30,000 books would explode to almost 68,768 in two decades?

Honest observers would agree that the war memorial committee and the library board showed some perspicacity when

116

they made what plans they did in 1950. It was Mrs. Kule's recollection that the library in the village hall was never significantly busy. The readership "explosion" came in the years after the Belmont library was in place.

Construction of the Arlington Heights Memorial Library was just ahead of the population swell. The electric wiring was completed in February, 1952. The heating system was ready except for a fluepipe between the boiler and the chimney. The furnace could soon go on. A charging desk and high swivel chair, round tables for the children's room, twenty-four reading chairs and rectangular tables for the adult readers, a magazine stand, a dictionary stand, and a Davidson book dolly were coming from Marshall Field's. The bronze plaques for the vestibule cost $105 each. The landscaping contract was let to H. Klopp. A commercial cleaning firm cleaned the windows and the building.

It was time to plan the grand opening. Daisy Daniels, the town historian who wrote *Prairieville, U.S.A.,* was asked to write a short history of the library. Taking its customary responsibility for rallying when needed by the library, members of the Arlington Heights Woman's Club planned refreshments for the open house for village officials, and officers of the American Legion, Veterans of Foreign Wars, Community Council, and the woman's club.

There were even to be new books, eight hundred dollars worth, for display at this auspicious gathering.

Meanwhile, back at the municipal building, Florence Kule and her two assistants were facing the task of dusting ten thousand books and sorting them into milk bottle cases tagged to indicate whether they contained fiction or non-fiction, children or adult, or reference books. It was a staggering operation, made more onerous by an unexpected early

June heat wave. "We had only a small fan," Mrs. Kule would recall.

Her daughter Pat Kule whom the board had hired for part-time work at one dollar an hour and Flavia Feind worked with Mrs. Kule through those warm June days and into the evenings, boxing the books and lining up the boxes on chairs by the window. When village employees backed the trucks to the window on moving day and hoisted their chute to the window ledge, the boxes of books slipped down as easily as schoolchildren on a slide. "We just gave those boxes a nudge," Mrs. Kule recalls, "and off they went down the chute."

This was only half the process. Like Henry Bolte who told for years how he handled every brick twice for the bank/ Sieburg's Drugstore/Countryside building, picking them up at the freight depot in downtown Arlington Heights and laying them out at the site of the building at 1 West Campbell, Mrs. Kule and her aids reversed the procedure, picking out of the milk bottle cases each book they had tucked in. Ten thousand of them, and not like Wordsworth's ten thousand daffodils "tossing their heads in sprightly dance." The books grew very heavy.

Adult books went to the south wing, children's to the north wing, the reference books into the stacks behind the charging desk, and Mrs. Kule's personal effects to the office in the southwest corner with her new typewriter desk and swivel chair from Marshall Field's. The change from the municipal building was dramatic, and somewhat overwhelming.

There were all those empty shelves. Before she had begun her strenuous dusting ritual, Mrs. Kule had described those wide open spaces to the sympathetic staff at the Illinois State Library. Even as carpenter-contractor William Hanke was dismantling the old shelving and reassembling it with the new at the Belmont location, state library people were choosing current fiction and library basics to fill the long gaps.

As the lilacs bloomed that spring of 1952, and the crocuses poked through the earth, builders gave finishing touches to the Bedford limestone on the facade entrance and the east windows and the coping course around the brick walls. Interested library-watchers could see the charging desk put in place in the spacious lobby and behind the desk the wooden book stacks with shelf room for twelve thousand non-existent books. There were plans to replace the wood stacks with steel later to double their capacity. That was certainly not yet needed.

Even with the truckload of books from the state library, some shelves looked as lonely as stretches of Scarsdale during the Depression when the utilities were in but the houses were not.

Library construction had been held up in the spring by a strike of cut-stone workers which threw the other contractors off schedule. Now the library open house was being pushed forward, also, to June 28.

However, the memorial library was a reality, a credit to the determined strategists who had envisioned a free-standing, stone-ribbed sanctum to house the culmination of the Ladies Reading Circle's dream in the cold winter of 1887.

Visitors at the officials' open house, and then at the public's, nibbled at cookies and punch provided by the women of the club and congratulated the library board on a building worthy of village readers. They commented on the vistas, looking north into the neatly draped children's room decorated in turquoise and south to the handsome new furniture from Marshall Field's in the adult reading room.

They had many to thank besides the board: members of the Arlington Heights Woman's Club who had campaigned

South reading room, Belmont

door to door with petitions for the eighty thousand dollar referendum; Veterans of Foreign Wars, the American Legion and the Community Council which accumulated the War Memorial Fund; U.S.O. funds returned to the village; business men, organizations, and churches which had supported the project.

The Monday after the open house, June 29, the library opened to a public which would continue to grow at what was, for librarians who had worked the desk at Vail and Davis, an incredible rate. In 1952 the population of Arlington Heights was approximately ten thousand. Almost one person in ten, 859, signed up for library cards in the first five months after the library opened the great doors in the Bedford stone facade.

By February, 1953, there were 2,600 card holders, and 4,000 by the end of the year. By 1954 the number of card holders had tripled in two years. When a representative of the Gaylord check-out system suggested to Mrs. Kule a change from their method of writing the number in each book and marking the card with a rubber stamp date, she went to the board. Once the new method was explained, Milton Burkhart was in favor. "Give the lady what she wants," he advised the board. The system was instituted for the adult check-out desk, and soon after for the children's.

In spite of the stunning increase in card holders and the concomitant work load, the character of the library continued true to Miss Effie's ideal of matching reader to book. "We broke our neck to find books people wanted," Mary Meyer reported.

The atmosphere continued to be friendly and informal, low-key and social. The women who checked out books at the big desk just inside the front door tended to be friends from the Methodist church. Like Mrs. Kule when she applied, they were women looking for a little extra money, a couple of evenings out a week, and an interesting environment.

They empathized with the patrons. Nathalie Wallace, who served as board president in the seventies, remembers her daughter losing a book when she was still so young that reading in bed at night was naughty, Mrs. Wallace went in to pay up. "We just can't find the book," she said. "I'll have to pay for it."

The librarian wouldn't hear of it. "Oh, these books always turn up," she said. "Don't pay for it. You'll find it."

When the book was found sometime later (the youngster had hid it between her mattress and box springs when she thought she was going to be caught), there was no charge. "We told you you would find it," the woman at the desk said. "Thank you very much." Mrs. Wallace felt like part of their community of friends whose delight was to pair books and patrons. Like the visitors at the 1952 open house, she was charmed by the child-sized round tables and chairs by the handsome big window in the children's section. Now she had an additional reason to like the library.

For the staff, the Belmont library was "the best place in the world to work." Mary Meyer liked every aspect of her day. "As far as friends were concerned, we were a very close group and our librarian was wonderful. So were our 'carriage trade,' our elite readers. They kept us on our toes, always wanting to read the newest books."

Although no one on the staff, except a temporary reference librarian, had any education in library science, many of them were avid readers. For Mary Meyer, who was a great fiction reader, it was an education to discover the breadth of the library's resources. "Often I would be the only staff member on hand," she recalls, "and I had to know what was available, and where. A lot depended on staff members." A patron might—as one patron did—ask for a book he needed for class written by "Orson Welles" with a title that was "all numbers."

Without comment the staff person gave him *1984* by George Orwell. Another staff person had to hold back a smile when a youngster asked for a book on the "bass and persecution instruments."

Stories like these circulated in the library, as well as books.

Sometimes a story originated there like *The Case of the Malodorous Aroma.* First noticed in the reading room, the odor was quickly traced to a closet in the south room where the magazines were stored somewhat haphazardly but with a charm that was inviting for someone who wasn't in any particular hurry to put his or her hand on a particular issue.

Staff members lugged one magazine pile after another into the main reading room without finding the source of the troubling odor. They washed the shelves and mopped the floor. Their pleasant library still smelled like the rotting fish—which the librarian discovered in a drawer in the small table in the closet. Evidently one of the children who had been "trout-fishing in the park" at the end of the swimming season had decided to share his catch.

This fish story, like many others, loomed larger than life because the daily routine, however friendly and social, had its tedious aspects. Juanita Conrad thought it was a nuisance, for instance, to have to sift through the little box containing names of delinquent patrons every time she checked someone out. What the members of the staff liked was working on their specialties, one at lettering, another at pasting the pockets in the books, another at cataloging. "Everyone was good at something," according to Florence Kule.

Board members also brought various and individual talents to the library. Paul Patrick, a grandfatherly-looking-and-acting man, was forever coming in to see what needed fixing. He was the man about the house, in a way, specializing in electrical maintenance. Robert Blackburn was appreciated because he took an interest in the staff's working conditions, suggesting that wages should be raised, that Social Security benefits and insurance should be instituted. The staff was grateful for the big box of candy he sent every Christmas and the party that Florence Hendrickson gave for the staff in her handsome lannon stone home on north Belmont.

The Belmont library outdid the Vail and Davis quarters in space and staff and volume, but it preserved the old town flavor. When the staff worried about secreting the cash overnight, they decided to fake a book, hollow to hold the money, with a pseudo-call number to make it indistinguishable from its shelf mates. Last thing every evening one of the staff would empty the cash into its night deposit-book. As one of those women thinks back now, "there was nothing to prevent a person looking in the window to see where we put it."

But who would do anything like that?

14.
Expansion On Belmont

"I loved the mornings." Florence Kule remembers the beginning of each library day as peaceful. "I could stay in my office and order books, or catalog them, or write articles for the Paddock paper about them.

"In fact, my office was the depot for new books."

As the voice of the bulldozer was heard all over Arlington Heights, chewing holes for new home foundations out of cornfields, the voice of Mrs. Kule was heard, deciding what new books the new home buyers would have to read.

Selecting as many as one hundred books a month was an arduous chore but, as Mrs. Kule says, "I had to do it. I ordered all the books for the library, all the fiction, all the non-fiction, all the children's books. Fortunately, I had found out about the American Library Association. I used the recommendations in their *Library Journal*.

"We never had any complaints about what was on the shelf. If people wanted books we didn't have, we would order them from the state library at Springfield and get them in thirty days. Otherwise, our orders were placed through a jobber, A. C. McClurg and Company. That's all they handled, books. When the truck came with all the new books, they landed in my office." Then the pleasant morning task of readying the books for the patrons began.

The board was as uncomplaining as the public. "I could go to the board for anything," Mrs. Kule recalls. "I can't remember that they turned me down on one thing. I never had to be afraid to say this or that, that we should be doing this or subscribing to that."

Impressed by all the help she received from professional library associations, Mrs. Kule got board permission to host librarians, assistant librarians, and presidents of library boards from Regions I and II of the Illinois Library Association, a first for the Arlington library. "It was a red-letter day," she recalls. Luncheon was served at the Methodist Church and board members helped with refreshments for 120 guests.

The board also agreed that Mrs. Kule should attend the ILA annual meeting in Springfield in the fall of 1954. They could see that whatever information Mrs. Kule culled from such programs would benefit all the library's patrons. In fact, it was absolutely necessary for her to develop her skills for choosing and deploying books. Two years before in the municipal building location, the library had about fifteen hundred readers. After the move to Belmont, more than one hundred persons signed up every month until in December, 1954, just two and one half years after the opening, there were five thousand users, more than three times as many.

The people in their ranch houses in the new subdivisions were doing more than seeding grass and attaching appliances. They were taking out five thousand books a month, including the hundred new books that Mrs. Kule was choosing.

That volume was somewhat overwhelming even though staff (now three assistants and two high school girls) was added so that two persons were at the check-out desk, except at lunch time.

Pleading the responsibilities of family life, Mrs. Kule approached the board about replacing her with a professional library director. The board, amenable to her suggestion, interviewed her candidate, a children's librarian who worked at the Edison Park branch of the Chicago Public Library. When the candidate hesitated because she would lose her pension benefits, Mrs. Kule agreed to stay on, on a four-day week basis. She also planned a two-month summer vacation for herself while her daughter Pat Kule, who had been a very useful assistant back at the municipal building library, would be home from college and willing to take over in her mother's office.

Those changes made the job more tolerable for Mrs. Kule and gave Pat Kule an opportunity to resume the children's story hour which had been introduced by Mrs. Baxter in the thirties and then dropped. Pat Kule's storytime was the beginning of permanent children's program planning.

Like the ridership on the North Western, the readership at the library climbed the charts. The 5,000 card-holders in December, 1954, were 5,575 five months later. Hundreds more trying to find parking places and blocking Reuben and Juanita Conrad's driveway next door to the library in their frustration. Hundreds more in line at the check-out desk. More bikes in the bike rack provided by the woman's club. More requests for keys to the lavatories. More patrons clamoring for bestsellers.

There were problems. One was the phone bill. Although children lining up to call home had boosted the monthly bill to ten dollars, the board decided it was not yet necessary to install a pay phone. Board members did decide, however, that it was time to raise the freight on non-resident users. In 1950 the non-resident fee was fifty cents; it was raised to two dollars in 1952 for now there were twenty users. By 1955 non-residents were eager to use the Arlington library facilities, partly because other libraries were upping their fees. The board agreed to hike the non-resident fee to five dollars a year. They also asked the police department for two-hour parking signs because the communters were taking the few spaces available for patrons.

Juanita Conrad loved being able to duck out of her house next door at one and half minutes to ten, slip through the hedge and take the stairs into the library at the very moment appointed for the start of her work day. It was another matter when she was trying to go anywhere else—at least during library hours.

"It seemed whenever we had an appointment or any reason to be on time somewhere that some library patron would have parked across our driveway. We'd have to go out, take down the license number of the car that was obstructing our drive, and then go into the library to find out who was preventing our escape."

It wasn't only the patrons' difficulty in finding legal parking places for their cars. By 1956 the librarians could find no places for books.

Like the quick-growing squash in one of the children's stories, the quick-growing library was crowding the alloted space. The unrelenting addition of books to the shelves, hours to the day, and patrons to the rolls was causing growing pains. The library board decided on a suburban solution— put the kids in the basement. Also, the magazine reading room.

That summer, as the last scheduled steam engine huffed and puffed out of Arlington Heights, the library board called in Walter Kroeber, architect, to talk about remodeling. They'd found out at their August, 1956, board meeting that not only was July a record month with nine thousand books checked out, but also there was some money available. There was eight thousand dollars on reserve at city hall and the eleven thousand dollars from new taxes they could use for renovation of the lower level into a children's department.

In 1952, when Walter Kroeber presented the statement on the building fund, $88,755.08 had been paid to date on the cost of the original building. He told the board that they had $3,900 left but their debts were $7,480. The library had to borrow $4,000 from the village which was repaid in December that year. The library's budget in 1952 was $15,500. Again the library was going to have to borrow from the village once its renovation was under way.

With the expansion of the children's library into the basement came an expansion of spirit in the person of Edith Lindsey whose elegant taste made her "absolutely superlative in her field," according to Mary Lee Ewalt, head librarian during the later years of Miss Lindsey's incumbency.

"A real book snob," Mrs. Ewalt added, describing how Miss Lindsey, who had already had an esteemed career as an English teacher, bought nothing but the best—"and she knew the best"—for the children who climbed down the stairs into her basement kingdom. Miss Lindsey's discriminating judgment strengthened the children's department immeasurably.

She had two fetishes, Mrs. Ewalt recalls. "First, she threw away all the Nancy Drew mysteries the library had accumulated." Other staff members objected that the books were harmless and might encourage young girls to read. Edith Lindsey was adamant. "The library doesn't have to have trash like that. If their parents want children to read that kind of book, they can buy them themselves."

What justified her unforgiving taste was her wide knowledge of children's books. "She was currently conversant with all children's literature," Mrs. Ewalt says. Edith Lindsey knew and loved the inestimable treasure buried in children's books, its potential for elevating the spirit, its power to explain the past and unlock the future.

She could not bear to weigh her shelves with the insignifi-

Head librarian Evelyn Stadelman with children's librarian Edith Lindsey

cant. She wouldn't let bad books, or even frivolous books, drive out good books. "She spoiled us," one of those young mothers who brought her brood to choose books every week in the fifties recalls. "I remember my anticipation at visiting the children's section of the Chicago Public Library on Michigan Avenue. I stood under those glorious Tiffany ceilings, my expectations soaring. If the Arlington Heights children's section could be so satisfying what could I not expect in this great city library?

"What I found out, of course, was that the Chicago collection couldn't compare with Arlington Heights'. Nor did the librarian have the same confidence in my children, telling us that they were too young for the Laura and Mary volumes we were requesting. We had already read three or four aloud which we had borrowed from Miss Lindsey's store. They were ready for Laura Ingalls Wilder."

Miss Lindsey's second idiosyncracy was tidy books. "Her books had to be physically clean. Once a year a team of high school students carted every single book into the little kitchen that served as a staff lounge and damp-washed the cover," Mrs. Ewalt tells. Then each of the books was neatly replaced for the satisfaction of the young patrons who also liked books clean.

Elinor Hackbarth remembers that during her days in the children's department Edith Lindsey was the "head of the library family." Whenever the staff gathered for a sociable treat of sweet rolls and coffee at the long table in the northwest corner of the building, Edith Lindsey at the head of the table "acted as our mama. She was always so jolly."

About the time that Florence Kule was contacting Edith Lindsey for the part-time job as children's librarian downstairs, changes were in the making upstairs. Florence Kule had found a replacement. She asked Evelyn Stadelman to work at the library part time, "even though I had no library experience," Mrs. Stadelman says today. "I did have a good foundation and experience in the field of purchasing, and my education was in business and religious education from Bethel Seminary in St. Paul, Minnesota."

Once Mrs. Stadelman had learned all the library procedures, Mrs. Kule was at last able to retire in her favor. Parenthetically, it should be noted that shortly after moving to Barrington with her family, Mrs. Kule applied for a position shelving books in the Barrington library. In short order, she was head librarian there.

According to Mrs. Stadelman, the Arlington Heights library board had advertised for a head librarian in the *ALA Journal*. But they couldn't afford the salary a professional asked. Mrs. Stadelman took several short term courses in cataloging and library procedure at the University of Illinois.

At that point all the employees were on a part-time basis, "mature women who were very conscientious, competent, and gave of their time beyond the call of duty," according to Mrs. Stadelman. She herself filled in as typewriter repairperson because she'd learned to take a typewriter apart in a repair course.

The staff also served as emergency crew. So did their families. When Juanita Conrad noted from her house next door water splashing in the library furnace room, it was Mrs. Stadelman and her son who rushed in to discover burst water pipes. Her son turned off the water. The two of them mopped floors, walls, and furnace.

When Evelyn Stadelman, "a lovely Methodist woman," took over in July, 1959, she told the board that there were items demanding attention: a malfunctioning police alarm, dripping pipes, broken windows, adjustments on the gas water heater, and a lack of towel racks in the men's room.

Those were minor problems compared to the July flood that ruined three hundred children's books. Mrs. Stadelman called "board members, her husband, and other staff members who came with boots, brooms, shovels to rescue what we could and sweep back the muddy waters into the drains. What a mess! We brought our own electric heaters to help dry out those books not too badly soaked, but many books could not be salvaged."

New registrations were coming in at a rate of 280 a month when Evelyn Stadelman took over. Mrs. Stadelman could see the need for dynamic leadership on the library board and went looking for it on the roster of the Arlington Heights Woman's Club.

Prior to her accession at the library, Mrs. Stadelman headed the Arlington Heights Woman's Club and served as chairperson of one of the departments of the seventh District of the Illinois Federation. Determined to augment the board's view of the library's potential, Mrs. Stadelman approached the woman who had succeeded her as president of the woman's club, Florence Hendrickson.

"Florence," the new librarian said, "you will have to run for the board of directors of the library."

"What?" a surprised Mrs. Hendrickson remembers replying.

"I've already put your name up," Mrs. Stadelman announced. "The library needs you. I need you."

Mrs. Stadelman recognized Florence Hendrickson as ambitious for her town and brimming with the energy to get projects accomplished. She knew the board required that indefatigable drive. Paul Patrick, whose service went back to Wing/Davis days, was very lowkey, beloved for his care and concern for the library. But he was not aggressive. "He was the kind of person who wouldn't speak unless he was spoken to," Mrs. Hendrickson says. "He was like our little handyman. Instead of calling an electrician who would charge the taxpayers thirty-five dollars, for instance, we would ask Mr. Patrick to tinker with the fixtures. It was wonderful to have him."

There was always some nagging repair needed: a broken

door jam, a plugged waterpipe, a burnt-out bulb. That was the little stuff. Then there were questions about whether to install a public telephone in the lobby. This idea was dropped because the telephone company asked a twenty-five dollar guarantee. The serious problem was the increase in readership traffic. Two hundred and fifty children signed up to read ten books as part of the Reading Club in the summer of 1957. A year later 539 signed on. That was one set of numbers on the tally for expansion.

There were others. The seven thousand users, up from fifteen hundred in five years. The need for a work area in the children's room. The need for space for hundreds of new books. The number of illegal parkers in the Conrad's driveway.

Expansion was discussed with the architect Walter Kroeber, including a tentative plan for a second floor in the stack room. When it was decided that in conjunction with the current remodeling an overall study of the library's progression should be made, Florence Hendrickson, Elsie Hubbard, and Robert Blackburn, a new member in 1958 and vice president of the Harris Trust and Savings Bank, were appointed to do the long-range study.

Meanwhile, changes and repairs at the Belmont location included the double decking of the central section of the building to increase the book storage capacity by twenty percent, complete redecoration of the interior and paving of the back parking lot.

The population in 1958, six years into the library's life, was already more than double Walter Kroeber's working figure of 10,000-12,000 in 1952. The number of books checked out at the Arlington Heights Memorial Library was more than double the number checked out in 1952 or 1953.

The library was expanding laterally. Five hundred books

were commandeered from the state library to furnish a summer branch at Pioneer Park. The library provided one thousand books, shelves, and the librarian Judy Grose. The park district contributed the supply room and other necessary furniture. An average of twenty-four children came to the daily story hour and an average of 124 scanned the shelves for summer reading. One hundred and fifty-nine enrolled in the summer reading club; sixty-eight read the required books.

Costs were rising so fees on rental books rose from three cents a day to a dime for the first three days, payable in advance, and five cents a day thereafter. The charge for reserving new fiction was ten cents, also payable at the time of reservation. Because a two-cent fine was no longer stiff enough to bring the books back in, the library raised the penalty to three cents.

The book population continued to soar. When the woman's club was hauling its annual Christmas tree into the library lobby in 1958, the aroma of balsam wafted toward twenty-eight thousand books. "They'd be stacked on the floor for lack of shelving space if they were all here at once," Mrs. Stadelman pointed out. The library let the contracts for the construction work in January and the work was begun.

By April Fool's Day the lower level of the north wing had been expanded to hold the books read by children up to eighth grade. Teen books were moved to the central area in the lower level. Part of the storeroom was remodeled into a lounge and workroom for repairing books, and Edith Lindsey got an office in the chidren's wing.

The library found itself in a financial bind. Spending in the Illinois tax system in the fifties was always a year ahead of the collection of tax receipts. The library had stayed within the limits of the budget it had created, but only eighty-five percent of the taxes were collected. The library ran short of cash with five months to go in the 1958-59 fiscal year. After discussion with the village finance director, the village authorized transfer of $30,000 to the library expense fund in lieu of $15,000 voted in March. This could be drawn on by the library in amounts of $5,000, as it was needed, at 2½% interest. When the library collected its taxes, the village would be reimbursed.

Actually, the county came through with the collected taxes before the library had to turn to the village. Village officials were grateful because they were building a new municipal building on Arlington Heights Road.

However, it was quite clear that the library needed additional funds to satisfy villagers' appetite for books. Presently, the taxpayers were giving .0651 per $100 of evaluation. The average house in Arlington Heights was valued at $27,000, assessed at $7,000, a third of its market value. The average family was paying $4.56 to support the library each year.

State law allowed libraries to tax at .10 per one hundred dollars of home evaluation. That would bring the tax on each household in Arlington Heights to an average of seven dollars, if the library had immediate plans to increase its annual budget to the maximum. The library had no plans for such a jump.

Their budget in 1957 was $20,657; in 1958, $45,050; in 1959, $54,150. The 1960-61 budget was what the Paddock paper called a "modest $61,150." Although the increase that would be appropriated by the referendum was only a couple of dollars per household, and then only if the library went to its maximum taxing power, yet the aggregate for the library would be substantial. And necessary. The existing tax levy had gone into effect when the library occupied one room and managed with one full-time and one part-time staff person.

The handful of people who were informed and concerned shivered in fear that residents would shrug off the library appeal as just another tax hike and spend the April Saturday digging leaves out of their flower beds and doing other spring cleaning.

The concerned few did what they could. The League of Women Voters invited head librarian Evelyn Stadelman and board member Robert Blackburn to an open meeting.

The ever-faithful members of the Arlington Heights Woman's Club beat the "suburban bushes," according to the *Arlington Heights Herald,* "calling on friends and neighbors, imploring strangers" to get out and vote.

It wasn't that townsfolk weren't using the library. They were coming in by the thousands. Over eight hundred children were enrolled in reading clubs at the two library locations that summer of 1960. Some of their parents must have appreciated that bounty.

Yet, only a saving remnant dribbled into the polling places at the municipal building and North School Saturday, April 30, 1960. Out of a village population of 28,000, there were 149 faithful friends of the library who voted to raise the levy. Fortunately only 37 voted "No."

15.
Decision To Move Again

An astounding three out of five villagers had library cards in 1963. Twenty-one thousand patrons found 212,000 books on the shelves that they thought they would like to read. The library had matured into a stable resource and substantial asset to the village.

Yet library negotiations retained the ingenuous, spontaneous air of early years.

As Mary Lee Ewalt recalls her accession to the post of head librarian in the early sixties, her story echoes Florence Kule's initial interview with board president Paul Patrick when the library was in one room. It is equally offhand.

Mary Lee Ewalt had checked out books part-time for about a year when, one evening "as we were closing," Mrs. Ewalt recalls, Evelyn Stadelman joined a cluster of staff members at the check-out desk. She inquired casually if any of the staff "knew anyone who wants to be head librarian here?" Charles Stadelman had been transferred to Detroit and the position would be open.

"I said, 'I do,' " Mrs. Ewalt remembers. Thus the royal succession was managed.

Actually, Mary Lee Ewalt's induction was "a little more formal than that," she recalls, "but not much. Mr. Dibble was president of the board then and I was interviewed twice by the library board. They offered me the position and I took it."

She explained to the board carefully that her experience

Head librarian Mary Lee Ewalt with a book donor

was in rare book cataloging, not library cataloging, but that caveat did not influence their decision to hire her. They made a sound choice. Mrs. Ewalt's experience working for rare book connoisseur Walter Hill, whose heart's delight was a hand-written copy of Jane Austen's *Sense and Sensibility,* whose specialty was Icelandic literature, whose appreciation for English literature was wide, had honed her taste to an acuity the Arlington Heights library was ready for.

Mrs. Ewalt was another book snob. Like Miss Lindsey she began to toss unfit books. It was a sore point with the staff.

"I didn't like the Readers' Digest Condensed Books," Mrs. Ewalt admits. "We had shelves of them. I didn't think they were quality acquisitions. I threw them out right and left."

Subsequently, she adds ruefully, "they were brought back." After her time.

Another category Mrs. Ewalt dislodged from its nest was the "tons of upward-and-onward books. I don't remember their titles. They were eminently forgettable. A lot of them were donated over the years. By the time I got to the library the acquisitions were supported by tax money, as they should be. We weren't entirely dependent on donations as librarians were in the old days.

"We could no longer afford the space to house books that wouldn't do the greatest good for the greatest number of people."

For instance, Mrs. Ewalt points out, schools were expanding rapidly. Students needed classics and reference books instead of "smile-and-the-world-smiles-with-you."

Mrs. Ewalt determined to provide the finest and most useful collection of books possible under the library's financial limitations. Even if the library did not have the money to buy every book she considered necessary, Mary Lee Ewalt did not accept donations of encyclopedias or textbooks that were out-of-date. Some patrons didn't understand, she admits. They'd paid dearly for these texts, maybe for their children. Yet she adhered to her stance that no information was better than wrong information. "If we didn't have it we didn't have it, but we did not give out wrong information."

Working along with Mrs. Ewalt, and sharing her office, Jo Running found the Belmont Avenue library a cozy little place. From the early sixties until the late eighties, Running was a bulwark of the library staff, taking minutes for the board, keeping tabs on the operation, always aware where 'the body was buried,' according to one of the board members.

Mary Lee Ewalt's availability for the executive librarian

140

job, whether by chance or serendipity, presaged a dramatic change in the library. While it was true that the board stumbled on Mrs. Ewalt by the time-honored gamble—"Know anyone who wants to be head librarian here?"—she had the education (a college major in history), the experience (fine book collecting and cataloging), the forthright administrative skills, and the keen intellect necessary to manage the imminent transitions.

Her leadership was one of the elements that was roiling the Arlington Heights Memorial Library to a flash point. There were others. As Mrs. Stadelman made her reluctant goodbyes in May, 1962, the board was electing Florence Hendrickson, Arlington Heights' greatest booster—"I think Arlington Heights is the greatest city in the country"—as the new president of the board.

Florence Henrickson is an original. Easily a thousand ardent villagers, from the earliest Chautauqua adherents to the Tri-Sigma enthusiasts through a series of staff and board members, struggled to create in their town a book collection which would be, as Thomas Carlyle said, "a true University." Only one looks out from a portrait in oil onto a handsome auditorium named in her honor. That is Florence Hendrickson of the Hendrickson Room.

The library was in the city hall, fifty feet from the tooting steam locomotives on the North Western tracks, when Florence and Clarence Henrickson chose the "little farmers' town" of Arlington Heights in 1945 because it "was so neat and clean. Those Germans, don't you know. They kept things up."

The owners of the sturdy Dutch Colonial residence at 303 North Haddow Avenue wondered why a young couple would choose their relatively spacious home. "My father always told me to get a big house in case there was another Depression

141

and people needed to move in with me," Florence explained. Asked by a newspaper reporter what they would do in Arlington Heights, she replied, "We are going into business." When pressed, she confessed that she couldn't specify what business. Nevertheless that is exactly what the couple did. And soon.

The realtor who sold them their house decided to retire to Florida shortly after they moved to town. Harold Willson offered to sell the Hendricksons Willson and Florence Realty for five thousand dollars. They made out the check. Three days later when the realtor tore up their check before their eyes and announced his new price was ten thousand dollars, the Hendricksons issued another. They never regretted their impulsive purchase.

"It was a great time for selling real estate," Florence Hendrickson recalls. "People were lined up every Sunday morning, trying to take those houses away from us. The $10,000 came back to us in two months."

While Clarence Hendrickson focused on selling real estate, Florence Hendrickson exerted an equal energy into animating Arlington Heights, "one of the greatest cities in the United States, a golden spot," as she often claimed. She had a finger in every pie, a foot in every door, and an opinion on every development. She did anything she could to help. She joined the Arlington Heights Woman's Club, which was meeting every month in the Recreation Park fieldhouse, and did all her work for the club from a desk in the real estate office. She collected for the Red Cross. She served on the Community Chest and the Community Concert Board.

"I've probably served on every board in Arlington Heights," Mrs. Hendrickson confesses. "I was too dumb to say 'no.' Anything that anyone asked me to do, I did," she adds, self-deprecatingly. She was Wheeling Township Committeewoman, receiving the "Republican Woman of the Year Award" in 1973, president of the Arlington Heights Woman's Club, and in turn, the Seventh District of Women's Clubs encompassing twenty-eight groups, the Northern Region Illinois Federation of Women's Clubs and, finally, the Illinois Federation.

She worked with Daisy Daniels, the author of the village history, during her term as president of the Arlington Heights Historical Society. She served on the Festival Committee for Frontier Days, and she was president of the Rotary-Anns, the women's division of the Rotarians. She received the Scouting Public Service Award from the Northwest Suburban Council of the Boy Scouts of America.

This force of nature was elected president of the Arlington Heights Memorial Library in May, 1962.

Additional components in the concatenation which would result in 1967 in the 45,000-square-foot magnum opus on Dunton Avenue were the architects Robert Nicol and Robert Chaney who, according to one board member, took on the library as a personal challenge and "contributed over and above what could be expected of architects paid to do a building."

Chaney saw a library expansion story in the *Arlington Heights Herald* one rainy Saturday morning and tooled his old MG convertible over to Florence Hendrickson's north Belmont address. According to Chaney, she answered his ring in curlers and a bathrobe ("only time I ever saw her not dressed up"), noticed the car ("I'd like to ride in one sometime"), and advised Chaney to write the board a letter expressing his interest in the project and outlining his firm's qualifications.

Later when Chaney's firm (Nicol and Nicol) was chosen after many lengthy interviews (because Mrs. Hendrickson was convinced his firm had the most experience in school and library building out of the six contenders), the board asked the architects to work out plans for an expansion of the present library building at Miner and Belmont. Four board members still favored expansion, not transplantation. The architects brought in handsome plans. Florence Hendrickson was aghast, according to Chaney.

Sensing that they had dressed up the wrong sister as Cinderella, Chaney and Nicol hastily pointed out that "with artistic license you can make anything look good in a drawing." Quickly back-pedaling, they allowed that the village could get by with the present building if villagers didn't mind their overwhelming addition giving the impression that the tail was wagging the dog. If the architects were charged to make the present building do, they could reinforce the floors, rearrange the stacks, create new traffic plans.

Floors that couldn't support the stacks were an issue. Librarian Mary Lee Ewalt had asked the architect of the Belmont building what the load limits of the floors were. "I really don't know," she recalled Kroeber telling her. Then could she move the stacks so the reference book stacks were at right angles to the walls?

"I wouldn't if I were you," Kroeber cautioned.

Actually, Chaney was pointing out that the stacks could be supported if there was additional reinforcement. But there were other factors militating against the Belmont location, at least in the minds of Florence Hendrickson and Mary Lee Ewalt. Five families would have to be dislodged for an addition. Parking was miserable. The location was out of the way.

Mrs. Hendrickson handed round a brochure on *Skillful Planning of a Library Building* to give board discussions more perspective. She appointed a site committee to work with village trustee Jack Walsh and planning commissioner Elmer Carlson.

The site committee resolved that two parcels of land, the present site of the library and the Dunton/Euclid/Vail/Fremont block, should be designated as possible library locations on the village master plan. A third possibility was the Miner/Douglas/Eastman/Hickory block just east of the present library. At the same time, funds were set aside for preliminary steps toward a library expansion referendum. In May, 1965, the architects, the village board, and the site selection committee had a joint meeting.

At least one villager complained in a letter to the local paper that the acquisition of new non-fiction was totally inadequate and that the use of paperbacks had only begun. He was convinced that if the library board would present the community with a program consonant with its needs, "they should have no difficulty in obtaining support."

Florence Hendrickson was determined to do just that. She saw her vision of a new centrally located library taking form in the public's imagination. She wasn't going to let board resistance cloud her determination because she was convinced that "there's not one thing you can't do if you make up your mind to it." Not waiting for fate to take a hand, she decided she would cash in some of her chits as a loyal advocate of village causes. Donning one of her distinctive handmade turbans, Mrs. Hendrickson set out to call on the town's major businessmen, people like Nick Lattof and Bill Poole and Carl Klehm, with whom she had served on village improvement committees for twenty years. She remembers telling them, "You've got to help me. You've got to put pressure on my board. Arlington Heights is at stake."

She recounted the months she had devoted to research, her

visits to suburban libraries around the county, her evaluation of their strengths and weaknesses, "what disasters they had built." She couldn't hold off the vote forever.

The businessmen were won over. Carl Klehm called board members and advised them simply, "I want you to let Florence have that library where she wants to." Other businessmen cooperated. Finally the forces supporting the Hendrickson/Ewalt vision were gathering together.

Two years of research, consultation, deliberation, foot-dragging and arm-twisting climaxed at the October, 1965, meeting of the Arlington Heights Memorial Library Board when, by a vote of three to two, it was decided that the board should start proceedings for an immediate referendum to purchase the block bounded by Dunton/Euclid/Vail/Fremont.

It didn't seem possible to some of the participants, who had grown discouraged, that the decision had finally been ratified. As Mary Lee Ewalt reflects on that momentous evening, she says "we went to board meeting after board meeting, the decision was hashed and rehashed, discussed and rediscussed, until, finally—out of sheer exhaustion, I think—the board decided that Dunton and Euclid should be the site."

When the jubilant board president came home to Clarence Hendrickson who had heard all the pluses counted and recounted, all the nays butted and rebutted, all the arguments refuted and confuted as his wife had worked out her strategy, she was triumphant. Clarence asked her how the meeting had gone. "Sit down," she charged him.

Almost before he could manage to obey, she blurted out her message of victory. "I won," she exulted.

The next morning, early, her phone rang. It was Mary Lee Ewalt, Mrs. Hendrickson's ally. Could Florence come over

146

for a cup of coffee? Just as Chaney had commented that only once had he seen the soignée Florence Hendrickson in less than formal garb, so Mary Lee Ewalt realized the significance of the occasion when the president of the library board appeared at the Ewalts' door in a housecoat. The two women analyzed their patient education of the board, citing this or that factor as the final goad toward the vote for a new library at Dunton and Euclid. In the end they conceded that they were puzzled at the success of their coup. "I was there," Mary Lee Ewalt allowed, "and I don't know how we did it."

"I don't either," admitted her confederate.

However they had done it, they had prodded the board into "thinking big," like their president. There was going to be a magnificent memorial to this vote, to the amplitude of the board's imagination, at the intersection of two main thoroughfares, just as the consultant had recommended.

Florence Hendrickson was invited for another cup of coffee before the week was done. Robert Nicol asked her to join him to talk over the board's decision and the library's future. What this architect, who had followed the evolution of the board's monument from a top-heavy doubling on Belmont to a lavish home for books at the confluence of two major streets, really wanted to do was to congratulate Florence Hendrickson for her vision and tenacity. "Florence," he said, "you were the only man on that board."

"Is that a compliment?" Florence Hendrickson asked.

"It is," the architect assured her.

16.
Planning The New Library

When Florence Hendrickson recruited Nathalie Wallace for the library board in 1961, Mrs. Wallace demurred. "I was a widow. I didn't want to leave my daughter home alone in the evening," Mrs. Wallace recalls.

Mrs. Hendrickson reassured her. The meetings were short, she promised. "Your daughter can read or study in the library while she waits for you. It's only a couple of hours once a month. We're always out by nine."

Mrs. Wallace pictured those inviting round tables, the little chairs and the low bookshelves that had charmed her when she first looked in on the library with her small daughter by her side. She agreed to a few hours once a month.

Florence Hendrickson did not misrepresent board habits. When Nathalie Wallace replaced the faithful Blanche Ashton (who was retiring after thirty years on the board—back to the days at the Peoples Bank), board meetings were brief and casual. Mrs. Wallace brought her daughter along and picked her up before she was restless. Only one night was there a mix-up when the meeting ran after nine. The librarian hustled young Miss Wallace and her friend out to the front steps to wait for her mother. The youngster had revealed that her mother was attending a meeting; she neglected to add that it was a library board meeting in the library basement. There were no further incidents.

It was fortunate that the young Miss Wallace was soon old enough to study home alone. For the short sweet candle of

Belmont board meetings burned at both ends once a new library was planned. After the leisurely rehashing, to use Mary Lee Ewalt's word, that culminated in the decision to build at Euclid and Dunton, there was to be no more leisure. The measured pace of those one or two-hour meetings lengthened in time and heightened in intensity. And were called with increasing frequency.

After the October decision there were November meetings on the ninth, the sixteenth, the twenty-third, and the thirtieth. The next month members gathered on the third, the ninth and the twenty-eighth, in spite of any other holiday arrangements. Nathalie Wallace remembers a Mothers' Day when, late in the afternoon, she finally said to a fellow board member, "Aren't you going to go home and wish Ellie a happy Mother's Day?"

The new community game which the board was playing was going to absorb their discretionary time for several years. There were simply far more decisions to be made. Another factor in the long board meetings was the addition to the board of George (Bud) Beacham, Jr., "bright as a dollar," as Mrs. Hendrickson said of him, and "willing to parley on every decision," as other participants recall.

Beacham came to the library board from the village board of trustees. John G. Woods, president of the village, turned his attention to the library as he did to every facet of the rapidly developing, increasingly sophisticated town of Arlington Heights. He "felt strongly that the library was one of the serious weaknesses in the community," according to a contemporary, and that some improvement should be fostered. He asked Bud Beacham and another dynamic young business executive on the village board to consider the library's needs, now that they were no longer going to run for the village board.

149

To persuade them, Woods took Beacham and Norval Stephens (the "Gold-Dust Twins," as Florence Hendrickson called them because they always sat together, thought alike and backed each other's initiatives) on an inspection tour of the library. They observed (1) the bad physical condition of the building, (2) the leaking roof, (3) the barely minimal facilities, and (4) the materials deteriorating from moisture. "I do not believe that Norval or I had any concept how bad the current library was," Beacham remembers. They agreed that in no way "did this institution fit the character of Arlington Heights as it was being developed at that time."

Beacham and Stephens formed a Citizens Committee to make the character of the library fit the character of the town. They themselves brought to it the expertise and information they had gained as members of the village board finance committee which dealt with the library budget. Under the law the library board set up its own budget, but the village board could refuse to pass the village appropriation and levy in which the library budget and tax were buried.

At the December meeting of the library board at which the resolution approving plans for the purchase of the Dunton/Euclid site, the erection of the library building there, and the furnishing of the building was passed, Norval Stephens explained how the building would be financed and where the funds would come from for books and extra operating costs. He also suggested that village manager L. A. Hanson, who had had an enormous amount of experience, should be construction manager for the new library, and that the Public Works Department of the village should move as much as possible from the old library to the new at no cost.

The estimated cost of the new library was $1,425,000, as follows:

Site	$114,500
Building	947,500
Equipment and furnishings	156,000
Architects' fees	72,000
Legal fees	15,000
Contingencies	120,000

There was no longer any question whether the new library was needed. Between three and four hundred persons applied for library cards every month. There were now more than fourteen thousand adults and ten thousand children registered at the library. "We really need the space," Mrs. Ewalt pointed out, adding "sometimes there is barely standing room in here." Actually, as Florence Hendrickson told Norval Stephens, the increase in book puchases was relatively small "because we don't have room for many more books."

As early as August, 1965, Florence Hendrickson had asked the park board to consider buying the existing library building, but the board refused because of "lack of information about next year's budget plus extension projects the park board faces." A negotiating committee composed of village president John G. Woods, village manager L. A. (Rudy) Hanson, and library board members Charles H. Oestmann and Robert Blackburn was going to have to search elsewhere for a buyer.

Top priority went to passing the $1,425,000 library building bond referendum planned for January 8, early in the year so that it would not conflict with a batch of elections that spring. Bud Beacham and Norval Stephens plugged their know-how and their know-who into that Citizens Committee formed to fetch an overwhelmingly positive base for the indispensable "yes" vote. What the voters were asked to approve was the issuing of $1,425,000 in bonds to build and equip a 40,000-square-foot library at Euclid and Dunton.

Plans for that library corresponded to recommendations from the Evanston-based Library Building Consultants that the new library be built on a through street that crossed the North Western tracks because most patrons would drive to the library, many of them across that natural barrier. By that standard the site was ideal; three of the bounding streets, Euclid, Vail, and Dunton, crossed the tracks. Other suggestions included abundant parking, possible on this 70,000-square-foot site (very close to the ideal of 75,000), and room for possible expansion, available at Dunton and Euclid, not on Belmont.

What the thirty-eight members of the Citizens Committee, fanning out into village meetings and gatherings, told the villagers was that the referendum would finance the site purchase, books and furnishings, architectural and legal fees for a building of 40,862 square feet. Of that total, 34,934 square feet would be finished by about the spring of 1967 (enough book space for a population of 57,000—13,000 over the present census), and the unfinished portion would be developed later to accommodate the expected surge toward a population of 75,000.

A villager writing the *Herald* that the book "collection is just too small for a city the size of Arlington Heights" touched on a deep concern of the committee. The library would have a building if the referendum was passed. How would it ever find enough books for all the patrons? That remained a question for the future. No one was willing to add a request for an operating tax rate raise to the present referendum for fear that the public would be intimidated by a brace of appeals. Yet the library shelved only one book per villager. Even if the board used a three-cent operating fund raise to fifteen cents per one hundred dollars evaluation, the library could only provide 1.9 books per person. Mature communities like Evanston and Wilmette had, respectively, three books per patron and six/seven. The average mature Illinois community had 2.5.

They would worry about book count, the committee decided, when they had convinced the public to roll out of bed one January morning and rally for the new low-lying, highly visible, centrally located book house. Advocates stressed repeatedly their message that the Belmont library was built in 1952 when the village population was 9,000, that the planned library would serve 57,000 patrons, that the building space would serve a projected maximum of 75,000 persons.

Construction costs were estimated in the $20-$22 per square foot range, commensurate with the costs of other new libraries. Because the Citizens Committee was frankly critical of the library books and services budget, the board agreed to increase its regular operating levy roughly two cents to the legal maximum of twelve cents per one hundred dollars of assessed evaluation.

Local writer Lester Ploetz prepared a report to the residents explaining that the Belmont library was only big enough to serve one third of the town's population, according to established library standards, had only a ten-stall parking area, and forced staff to use a hand-operated rope pulley to haul books up from the basement. Village president John Woods forcefully supported the referendum, urging villagers to "act now, before the deficiency of books and library services becomes critical."

The energetic collaboration between village groups was synergetic. Villagers heard the library story and were convinced that the solution was a whole new layout. When the 2,613 votes were counted on January 8, 1,977 were marked "Yes."

When an elated Florence Hendrickson announced that "we've taken a long time to put this package together," she was thinking of the immediate referendum. But, in a larger sense, that triumph of the library board, the Citizens Committee, the villagers who volunteered as judges, and the voters, was the triumph of a cavalcade of library workers trailing all the way back to Elizabeth Walker and her group taking the Chautauqua course. The library was the work of many hands, many hearts, many minds, all sharing a part of this day.

In the report after the election, Mrs. Hendrickson praised the "absolutely tremendous job" of the library Citizens Committee, noting that the board "couldn't have found two better men" to head the effort than Norval B. Stephens and George C. (Bud) Beacham.

That January there were three further developments. The elementary school system in Arlington Heights agreed to buy the Belmont library building. The village agreed to lend village manager Rudy Hanson as project manager for the construction of the new building. The library began to acquire books in anticipation of the move "one year from the day of the referendum," as Mrs. Hendrickson promised when the vote was counted.

Another major change was the resignation from the board of James E. Wood, who had decided to move to Oxford, Wisconsin, on his retirement from Montgomery Ward. Norval Stephens slipped into that slot, appointed by the board to serve until the next general election.

Now the various players in the new library drama took up their divers roles and duties.

Librarian Mary Lee Ewalt had her eye on the new building. With architects Robert Nicol and Robert Chaney, and sometimes board member Robert Blackburn, Mrs. Ewalt

154

traveled as far afield as Elgin, Gary, Elkhart, South Bend, and Waukegan, at the suggestion of library consultant Donald Beane, to study layout, use of study carrels, smoking policies, traffic patterns. The libraries they visited all had populations similar to Arlington Heights' because, as she said, "it wouldn't be much help to visit libraries that are much larger or have a different kind of clientele."

Mrs. Ewalt remembers a certain camaraderie among the day-travelers. Nicol was the scheduler, keeping everyone scurrying from appointment to appointment, not slating enough time, from Mrs. Ewalt's point of view, for an occasional sortie to the ladies' room. Asked about the head librarian's relationship with the board, she described it as relaxed, citing one of the rounds in the library excursions when she'd lagged behind the group, looking around for herself. Bob Blackburn, the link between her and the dashing architects, called back over his shoulder, "Hurry up, Toots, or we'll miss the next show."

While Mrs. Ewalt and the architects were focusing on the new library, the village attorney was negotiating to buy the site. The two handsome nineteenth century homes on the Dunton/Euclid/Vail/Fremont block were not architecturally unique (Bob Chaney called them "carpenter Gothic" as a shorthand for expendable). Both did have a rich village history, however. The Queen Anne home built in 1894 on the south end of the three-quarter acre plot was erected for one of the village's biggest employers. Richard Bray started making milk cans in the back of a hardware store he owned with Anthony Kates at 8 North Dunton (where William Dunton had once done business). In time Bray and Kates' sideline became their business. They built a factory just south of the Chicago and North Western Railroad at Ridge Avenue in

Bray-Whipple House

1897, three years after the family manse went up on Dunton. In 1966 that house was empty.

The Heller house on the north end of the block (which had once belonged to Bray's partner Anthony Kates) was not empty. Rosalie Heller, who worked part-time at the Belmont library, had shared the twelve-room, ninety-five-year-old house with her sisters since 1920.

It took the village attorney months of negotiation to work out contracts satisfactory to both families. When the contracts were finally signed in June, 1966, six months after the referendum, Mary Lee Ewalt found it hard to believe that the purchase had been completed. "It's wonderful to finally get it

Heller House

off the ground," she said. "Now I feel like we are really getting something done." The opening and awarding of bids on the $1,425,000 in bonds that the village board had approved could now begin on July 5 at the municipal building.

While Mary Lee Ewalt and the architects studied libraries and library plans, while the village attorney brought the Brays and the Heller sisters to the bargaining table, the library board studied the possibility of help from the federal government. R. Marlin Smith, acting attorney for Jack Siegel when the house contracts were signed, analyzed the method of applying for a federal grant for the purchase of books under Title 1 of the Library Service and Construction Act. To get those funds, the board had to provide working drawings of the new building and a timetable for construction. Once the board had plans, they could accept bids on construction and let the contracts by November 20.

All these decisions meant meetings. Nathalie Wallace who was wooed to the board on the promise of a short meeting once a month attended meetings on December 20, December 22, and December 27 of Christmas week, 1966.

As he moved that the December 27 meeting be adjourned, Bud Beacham suggested that the board should gather again on January 5.

17.
Differences Of Opinion

When Shakespeare's *Titus Andronicus* begs his daughter Lavinia, "Come, and take choice of all my library/And so beguile your sorrow," she is not to be comforted. Overwhelmed by disfigurement and grief, she cannot find in words the solace and enchantment that can be healing to those less mortally hurt. And yet the invitation stands, testament to Shakespeare's understanding of the power of books.

From its earliest days in the Shepard sisters' living room, the Arlington library issued Titus' invitation to the community: Come, beguile your sorrow, your joy, your thirst to know, your yen to learn, your need to inquire, your hunger to understand. Mrs. Baxter in the city hall library who "made friends with the kids," Edith Lindsey who would buy them nothing but the best, staff members who greeted patrons with, "We have a new book we know you'll love," all sought to beguile clients to readership.

Architect Bob Chaney picked up on this motif in his onset interview with head librarian Mary Lee Ewalt. She told him that, given her druthers, in the new library all the shelves would be on the outside of the building, the charge desk would be eliminated, and the patrons would take books as they pleased and return them at their leisure.

Secure in this generous mirage, Chaney was free to fashion inviting space: seating throughout the library convenient to stacks where patrons would be working, coffered lighting providing high light level with no glare, accessible and comfortable furniture to abet browsing and study.

Another facet of the ungrudging vision available to the library was Bud Beacham's belief that board members planning for the new building should "shoot for the moon and see how close we can come. Once we have an appropriate concept we can see if the community can afford it."

As Beacham and Florence Hendrickson rang doorbells and passed out literature for the library referendum, they touted the planned library as potentially "the cultural center of Arlington Heights." For Mrs. Hendrickson it was clear that "one of the most outstanding cities in the United States" should have "one of the most outstanding libraries in the United States." She saw the building as a monument. "I've always had the enthusiasm to build for future generations. I feel I was put on this earth to do something, not to sit and play bridge. There's something in me that I want to serve people, to leave something here."

While a visitor to a board meeting during the negotiations couldn't believe the length and intensity of the board's discussion of practical doorknobs for the new library, to the board members every aspect of the Dunton Street monument was of singular importance. A contemporary noted that Bud Beacham applied himself to the library as vigorously as another person would to a career.

Beacham thought library constantly, even through a surgical bout, ordinarily a rest from daily affairs. Architect Bob Chaney remembers riding the North Western one morning with Beacham who asked Chaney if he was making a bid on a library job in Chicago. "Architects don't make bids," Chaney explained. "They are professionals who make presentations to boards on the basis of their past performances. They don't bid against one another as contractors do.

"Being an architect," Chaney continued, "is like being a doctor or a lawyer. For instance, if you were getting your appendix out, you wouldn't go out and get bids on the operation."

"As a matter of fact," Beacham assured the surprised architect, "I just did exactly that. And you'd be amazed how much money I'm saving," he added, scuttling Chaney's point while illuminating Beacham's bulldog tenacity in getting the best possible deal.

During his recuperation Beacham asked no reprieve on library duties. According to Nathalie Wallace, he scheduled meetings at his house every day and parceled out his whole downtime. "I don't think he ever wasted a minute."

Beacham and Mrs. Wallace were part of a board that gave Chaney total cooperation. Some boards pull apart, some together, Chaney says. "The Arlington library board was always good to work with."

Busy as the board was going over specifications, dealing with the architect, picking the furniture, discussing specialty items, there was still a modicum of time left for politicking. One evening before the move to the Dunton Street library, Bob Blackburn advised Florence Hendrickson that the two young "eager beavers," as she called them, (by now Beacham had been appointed to replace the retired Elsie Hubbard) were contriving to wrest the presidency of the board from her by electing Beacham.

As she tells the story, Blackburn asked Mrs. Hendrickson to leave the next meeting so that he could explain to the board his strong feeling that Mrs. Hendrickson deserved to be president when the new library was dedicated. He pointed out how she had remained steady and hopeful during the time when four board members resisted the idea of a move. She had visited libraries and interviewed architects. She had

161

trudged from door to door with literature to persuade residents to pass the enabling referendum, brought the business community to the library's side, and rallied the Arlington Heights Woman's Club. The vote went three-three, then four-two in favor of Florence Hendrickson.

Nothing more was said of replacing Hendrickson. Beacham and Stephens remain, as Mrs. Hendrickson says, "two of my greatest friends until this day." The board could now get back to business.

When Beacham first saw the building plans designed by the architectural firm of Nicol and Nicol, he was disappointed, comparing the planned library to "any office building downtown," complaining that the building would not be more unique.

Other board members, satisfied that the textured limestone siding (achieved by dropping BBs between the sawblades as the stone was cut) and the landscaping would distinguish the building, turned to other areas of concern which could not be dispensed so quickly: the disposal of the two Victorian houses on the site, the possibility of federal financing, and the question of membership in the North Suburban Library System.

The most agreeable destiny proposed for the Heller home was removal to another site where it could serve as a historical museum. Unfortunately, a museum professional fixed on the Muller home at Vail and Fremont as more substantial and suitable. So the houses would go to the wreckers. But not before Arlington Heights residents had their chance to say good-bye. The library board generously agreed to tours, to a rummage sale, to an art fair, and to an auction of the fittings.

Books left in the houses were offered first to the library, then to the historical society which also received fireplaces, chandeliers, and mouldings from the homes. Between fourteen and fifteen hundred persons from places as distant as Florida, California, and Czechoslovakia toured the homes under the auspices of the historical society, examining the oval stained glass windows, the carved fireplaces, the original gaslight fixtures.

Members of the Arlington Heights Woman's Club and two Questers groups planned the house decor and dressed in turn-of-the-century styles to direct visitors in the two houses soon to be demolished for $2,800. Virgil Horath and Daisy Daniels, who knew as much history as anyone in town, stood around in the October sunshine to answer inquiries. The historical society raised five hundred dollars toward their new building.

The HN Chapter of the P.E.O. sisterhood managed a rummage sale in the Bray house, giving customers another chance to climb the front stairs. Then the Countryside Art Center, using welcoming boards (ironing boards decorated by local artists) as come-ons, displayed mobiles, pottery, oil paintings, watercolors, and pastels among the round turrets, hand-carved newel posts and storied halls of the three floors of the pioneer businessman's home. Before the display month was out residents could see exhibits by the Salt Creek Questers, the Dunton Questers, the Garden Club, and the St. James Junior High. There were antiques, pictures of old-time events, Civil War mementos, quilts, old-fashioned toys, stamp and coin collections, a flag exhibit, a rock collection, and a Founders' Room set up to show the early days of churches, parks, newspapers, and businesses in town.

Visitors at any of the events could keep an eye out for some artifact in the house that they might like to buy at the sealed-bid sale before the demolishing. Not only were there antique door and fireplace fixtures, there were also a relatively new water softener and garage.

The historical society made two hundred dollars on the thousand people who toured the Heller house, and sold 1,145 pieces of penny candy.

Once the owners of the Bray-Whipple and Heller houses agreed to a price, the disposition of the houses was more or less routine. This was not the case with the federal funding which was contingent, as Bob Chaney pointed out, on the library's answer to official queries on their position vis-a-vis the developing library system in northern Illinois. The library had made some overtures toward this operation; in early 1966 the board approved a resolution of intent to join the library system approved by the legislature that past summer, which would use state funds to set up a reference center and interlibrary loan.

Each step in the operation was contingent on another. The board could not apply for federal funds (through the state) until they had signed their contracts for the Bray-Whipple and Heller houses. They couldn't apply for the federal funds until they had agreed to join the North Suburban Library System. This was a real stumbling block. Believing that the public trusted them to make a decision about the interlibrary system (having voted for them), three board members voted to join the system at a meeting in September, 1966.

Bud Beacham was extremely upset when he heard about the vote. "It is regrettable that I was unable to attend the meeting," he said. "I am flatly opposed to joining the system and I wish I could have been there to make my ideas known."

Only Norval Stephens had voted against the opportunity to join the system at the meeting Beacham missed. While the other board members viewed membership in the system as a ticket to federal grant-in-aid, Beacham was convinced it was

164

more important to stay independent than to get federal money. He thought a common borrower's card would be developed to extend service to unincorporated areas and place an increased burden on facilities like Arlington Heights'. He could see that not every neighboring community supported a library equal to Arlington Heights'.

"I do not feel that I have a right to make a decision on behalf of the community to subject our library potential to state control," Beacham asserted. Calling the ploy "blackmail," he argued for asking Arlington Heights voters for the $400,000 that the federal funds would come to. "The decision was obviously made in the context that if we don't join, we don't get a federal grant," he said. "This is blackmail in its rawest sense."

Beacham sincerely believed that citizens would rather pay up than knuckle under and lose their autonomy. He was not necessarily against the concept of membership in a regional system. He could see that there would be benefits, but only "if and when we are assured the authority to choose our own destiny."

Those organizing the system understood the problem. Granting that the aim of the program was to provide small libraries the opportunity to make use of materials they couldn't afford, organizers admitted that "no library can be expected to loan materials in day-to-day demand in its own area of service." The interlibrary system was proceeding tentatively, having recently received its establishment grant. No one was certain how the system would deal with the information glut of the sixties and seventies. The times were new and so were the possibilities.

Advocates saw the potential. Any reader in the North/ Northwest suburbs would immediately find one million

Arlington High School students box books

books at his/her disposal. The plan coming out of the Library Development Committee of the Illinois Library Asso-

166

ciation posited daily delivery of materials. A central facility for getting information out to patrons seemed a necessity to deal with the information explosion.

Even so, none of the board members liked what they felt as pressure from the state librarian. All agreed that a common card would strain facilities. But Florence Hendrickson and Nathalie Wallace pointed out that it was perhaps the wisest course to join the plan and assure the obtaining of federal funds as no one knew whether common cards were a certainty or not.

Beacham was adamant, fearful of the control of the state librarian. "I will exercise every effort to reverse the decision of the board (made on September 22 to join the system). I will make use of every parliamentary maneuver available to me to see that the community has the opportunity to make a decision in this matter."

When the vote came up for the second time, Charles Oestmann, who was against joining the system (with Beacham and Stephens), agreed to leave the meeting, thus abstaining from voting, after the first vote had gone three-three to rescind the decision. Without his vote, the vote to join the system passed.

Beacham reiterated his plea that the decision be taken back to the voters. Nathalie Wallace disagreed. "I feel that we were elected to make other decisions," she said. "I believe that we are responsible and that we have been elected and that the community has faith in us."

The way was open. The library board airmailed a completed application for funds to the Illinois State Library Board. In November the library was promised a grant for $268,055, the full amount requested.

It was now time to interview contractors and to settle the question of the copper beech.

18.
Breaking Ground On Dunton

The hundred-year-old tree on the southwest corner of the Arlington Heights Memorial Library's new site was not a copper beech at all. But facts have never deterred romance even when the love object is a deciduous plant thirty feet tall.

Suddenly everyone in Arlington Heights loved the pseudo-copper beech. The village was losing two of its few distinguished homes. The public fastened on the irreplaceable tree as a proxy for the historic buildings.

The phone rang constantly at the Belmont library. An anguished voice would ask, "You're not going to cut down the copper beech?"

"No," Mary Lee Ewalt would answer patiently. "We are not going to cut down the copper beech." And the phone would ring once again. An anguished voice.

"They drove me nuts," Mrs. Ewalt recalls. "I began to think, 'Woodman, spare that tree.' I was so tired of getting phone calls about that tree. It was a sore point for me."

Not even an article in the *Arlington Heights Herald* quoting local nurseryman Carl Klehm to the effect that the tree at Vail and Fremont was a common American beech staunched the flood of phone calls and tearful pleas.

Klehm assured the library board that the gray, smooth-barked tree was quite rare ("I know of no other American beech of this size within the village"), and that it would not be hurt by construction if a thirty-foot circle was undisturbed around the tree.

The Heller sisters had made saving the beech a stipulation before they agreed to the sale of their home. The architect was comfortable working around it. The public was reassured. Gradually the phone calls rang down.

The public's interest now swung to the interesting question of the new library's construction. In the flush of victory at the success of the January, 1966, referendum, Florence Hendrickson had promised the voters a Dunton Street library one year hence. Construction was not that easy.

Only when the state had agreed to allot the $268,055 in federal funds to the Arlington library could the board open bids on the construction contract. Of the ten construction firms that submitted bids on the work only eight produced bids early enough to be qualified by the library board. A greatly relieved board was cheered when bids came in more than $100,000 below expectations. "When I opened that first bid, I knew we were okay," architect Robert Nicol commented.

With one change—that led later to a long-drawn-out court case—the board awarded the contract to Four Contractors, Inc., of Waukegan, the apparent low bidder at $1,148,689. Board member Bud Beacham estimated that the new building was going to cost about $28.50 a square foot when finished, $6.50 a square foot more than the original figure used when the bond referendum was passed in January, but $1.50 a square foot less than the price used to compute the total cost when the board applied for the federal grant in the fall.

There was a delay awarding the contract because Four Contractors requested permission to change one of their four sub-contractors. The firm hadn't had sufficient time to check out their electrical sub-contractor, who was alleged to have Mafia connections. According to Chaney, discussing the incident later, Robert Nicol slipped by alluding to the sub-contractor's objectionable ties at a meeting attended by a newspaper reporter. The resulting lawsuit dragged on for years until settled for a minimal sum.

Once the contractors had replaced their questionable supplier, work could start. For all the board's enthusiasm and diligent drudging at the details, Florence Hendrickson's promise of new construction in January, 1967, was a rosy fancy. The library board yielded a collective sigh of relief when they broke ground for the building on the day when they had hoped to fling wide the portals of "that solemn chamber" in which, as the English divine George Dawson noted, a person "may take counsel with all who have been wise, and great, and good, and glorious" among those who have gone before.

Actually, board members felt fortunate to be breaking ground. January 8, 1967, was a bitter winter day, not unlike the glacial afternoon four score years before when Elizabeth Walker had first gathered her friends into a ladies' reading circle a snowball's throw from the site of the 1967 ceremony. A spot of ground was cleared of snow. The president of the library board, the head librarian, the village president, and the village manager who was project manager on the library construction, wielded the shovel to scratch some earth from the frozen ground. A half hundred sturdy supporters stood with the other library board members to hear Florence Hendrickson, in a spirit of ardor and relief, call the day "one of the most significant in the history of Arlington Heights."

Satisfied with their year's work and confident in their project's value to the community, the board and elected officials repaired to the Hendricksons' for Swedish hospitality—and to get out of the cold.

Now it was appropriate to talk again about the need for more money to run the library they had broken ground for.

Bud Beacham predicted a much higher library tax rate and, by late 1968, a referendum to increase the library levy ceiling. There simply had to be more money to buy books for the increasing population of the village. Anyone could see that the new library was going to cost more to operate than the old one on Belmont. Already the 1967-68 budget for $208,000 included $100,000 for salaries, an increase of $17,000. Building maintenance was going up from $3,000 to $10,000; insurance from $3,000 to $5,000. The book budget was almost $60,000—four times what it had been a couple of years before.

Yet the book budget was a nagging insufficiency. As Beacham and Norval Stephens explained the budget rationale to the public that spring, their formula for funding was a slight increase in tax support and a bonding commitment endorsed by the village government. They knew this would produce a beautiful physical facility, according to Beacham, but that building would "woefully lack books. There seemed to be no way we could quickly make up for years of neglect."

Beacham sensed that the public would balk at another tax increase. What was needed was long-term financing to pay for the books that would make the library more than a beautiful shell with no body of learning within. Turning to the local state representative, Eugene Schlickman, Beacham began to research the possibility of changing state laws so that books could be purchased under the library and equipment bonds rather than through current budgeting.

Once he had a report from his staff on the pertinent statutes, Schlickman assured Beacham that there was no way under state law to solve the long-term financing of library books.

"Okay, Gene," Beacham countered, "then it's time to change the law. Let's draft a law you can sponsor to change

171

all this." They went to work on it immediately. By September, 1967, Governor Otto Kerner had signed a bill permitting libraries to hold referenda to buy new books.

Beacham said later that "had it not been for Gene Schlickman and his securing the governor's signature, we wouldn't have the library we have today." While they were about it, Schlickman and Beacham worked on an additional piece of legislation to add a member to six-member library boards. Twice in recent years the Arlington Heights Memorial Library Board had had crucial three-three votes, one over the much-contested decision to join the North Suburban Library System and another when Henrickson and Beacham tied for the position of president of the board. As Norval Stephens grumbled the night of the presidential vote, "Libraries are the only known boards in the state with an equal number of members." The addition of a seventh member would make voting less fractious, more clear-cut. Governor Kerner also signed that bill.

Public interest in the library emerged in actual library races for the four vacant seats in the April, 1967, elections. Incumbents Nathalie Wallace and Bud Beacham ran for—and won—the seats they held. Charles Edward, assistant to the present of Commerce Clearing House, Inc., came on board with Richard Frisbie, a self-employed advertising consultant and author of six books who had worked as a writer and editor for the *Chicago Daily News* for seven years. Frisbie was the third published author to serve on the library board, following Nathaniel Moore Banta and John Beaty.

That spring of 1967, in the upgrading spirit of the day, the library board approved a policy of linking pay raises to performance. Employees with below-average performance would receive a raise of about three percent while outstanding employees would receive a ten percent adjustment. Ac-

172

cording to Bud Beacham, the "merit system and the raise schedule is intended to attract professionals with good records," and to encourage full-time personnel rather than part-time personnel—a staple of the library from its very inception.

As they made their tours of surrounding libraries—once in a record-breaking blizzard—board members and library personnel picked up on interesting possible innovations. The library co-architect Robert Chaney and Mary Lee Ewalt noted a kind of central vacuum system in the Niles library that offered the feasibility of daytime cleaning instead of nighttime operation when the help would be more expensive. It was extremely quiet compared to the average vacuum. That was installed in Arlington Heights.

Beacham suggested that one way of forestalling creeping graffiti which germinated on washroom walls was installing stainless steel partitions in the lavatories. The board agreed that the extra three thousand, five hundred dollars would be well-spent.

According to Chaney, Beacham also urged on the board a custom-made stainless steel boot box on wheels which could be trundled out in inclement weather. The actual receptacles for the boots and galoshes were laminated plastic.

Perhaps the most charming innovation was a story pit for the youngsters who had been coming to story hour since Pat Kule introduced that pleasant library ritual on Belmont. The carpeted ledges created a bantam amphitheater where the storyteller could enclose his/her audience in a snug small world of their own. (It was lost to the below-ground parking in the first large addition.)

Going into the new library meant hiring additional staff, the head librarian pointed out to the board in March, 1967. Mrs. Ewalt admitted that it would be possible to run the

Story pit

library with the present staff. "But we cannot operate at the level of service which we should provide," she said. "And which the community is expecting us to provide in return for their investment," Beacham added.

When board members circled the village telling their story of library expansion before the April, 1967, election, residents had a chance to sight on some of their targets. They gave high priority to a quiet reading room. Library Building Consultants, Inc., came to the April meeting with a plan to chop up the patron reading room and to chop out the patron office space. The library board exploded. Beacham was "totally and utterly upset." He insisted that the board had spent hours and hours on their plan and "now a piece of paper from a consultant changes it."

He was not alone in his dismay. Before the evening meeting was over the board had compromised on a 572-square-foot quiet reading area which would seat approximately fifteen people and a typing room for patrons. Overall seating was for 240 persons. The current plan would house 87,000 volumes on the main floor open stacks, and 28,000 in closed basement stacks. The goal was 200,000 volumes with 50,000 always in circulation. The head librarian in the new $1.4 million building would get a raise to $9,000.

Anyone who had second thoughts about the expense of the new library forgot them when four inches of rain that fell in one and a half hours inundated the village in early June. Water backing up in the rear stairwell of the Belmont library forced open the basement door leading to the boiler room. After reaching a height of two or three feet in the boiler room, the water pushed open another door leading to the main part of the basement. The entire lower shelf of books around the walls was soaked beyond repair. Officials estimated the loss as at least one thousand books. Village manager Rudy Hanson declared that such a phenomenal rain occurred once in a hundred years. But library board members could recall enough similar emergencies to be glad that, while the foundation of the new library building was also under water, they did not expect to lose books there at some future date.

Mrs. Ewalt was not going to miss the cramped and drowned quarters at Belmont. She had no place to put books. Some were stored in the village hall. She had no place to put additional staff. As it was, she often served as reference librarian herself in the evening hours, answering difficult questions for patrons. She had to work from a regular library table. On occasion, when she would get up to find a reference for some fact she didn't have at hand, she would find her seat preempted by a patron who could find no other seat in the crowded library.

She tried to keep that personal service traditional back to the earliest days in the Peoples Bank, the days when "we knew the patrons, their names, their favorite authors or subject matter," as Evelyn Stadelman remembers. But sometimes the will to please approached the ludicrous. One late evening when a caller insisted that he wouldn't be able to get to work the following morning unless he had an auto manual to show him how to put his tire on, Mary Lee Ewalt met him at the back door after the library was closed to hand over the information. "I felt like I was running a speak-easy," she said.

She knew moving day was coming because the people from School District 25 who had bought the building were increasingly underfoot. As she explained it to the board, "You know, when you sell your house and the new lady comes to measure for curtains. Well, District 25 is in here all the time."

As District 25 measured at Belmont and Miner, library board members were fitting their furniture into the Dunton Avenue picture. Having got a low bid of $132,217 on their equipment for the new library, the board had a discretionary $17,149 to complete the furnishings. Several library board members traveled to the Merchandise Mart in Chicago to evaluate the appropriateness and durability of the furniture recommended by the architects. They had only seen pictures of the equipment. They wanted to put it to the Goldilocks test, to find out if the furniture was "just right" for the patrons who would be arriving in a few months. Chaney had picked furniture that eliminated the "leggy look" that he had seen in many libraries. The reading tables he'd selected had laminate plastic tops and ends that were gently rounded to allow for more seating and to avoid sharp corners. All the wood items had a walnut finish and the upholstery was Naugahyde.

What tickled the imagination of the taxpayers was the recommendation that the library buy a "womb chair," designed by Eero Aarnio of Finland, for $729. The local paper called this upholstered fiber glass shell which swiveled on a

"Womb chair," occupied

steel base "a refuge from trauma." Many of Florence Hendrickson's callers suffered trauma at the thought of the library spending $729 of the taxpayers' money for the controversial 007 lounge chair. Florence was sympathetic. "I am a practical person," she said, promising that she would never vote to bring the chair into the library.

The *Arlington Heights Herald* suggested that the womb chair was "functional sculpture," proposing that residents "who have been chafing at the accusation the suburbs are the final nesting place for middle-brow Philistines" could point with pride to the "far-out" chair in the library. Frisbie could see the public relations aspect of the chair. "It will bring people into the library and when we want to draw attention to the library it will be available for photographs."

Board members more interested in taxpayer relations than public relations were adamant, although Nathalie Wallace finally said she would be glad to see the chair as a gift.

In a sense, it was. Maintaining that the architects felt "the library wouldn't be the same without it," Chaney announced at the June board meeting that the architectural firm would pick up the difference—$405—between the womb chair and an ordinary lounge chair.

The board paid $323 and were happy. The public is happy to this day. "It's never empty," a library staff person says. "It even served for a while as a mini-apartment for a man who used to turn it to the wall and perch in it every day.

"He'd push it near an outlet so he could plug in his electric razor."

19.
Empty Shelves

Resplendent in one of her distinctive turbans, Florence Hendrickson fidgeted at the podium set up for the dedication of the new Arlington Heights Memorial Library. It was Sunday afternoon, June 30, 1968. Village officials, guests, residents, library board members stood in little knots, commenting on the sultry weather, the relative comfort of the under-roof parking lot "auditorium," their general satisfaction in their new library.

Mrs. Hendrickson could see the village president chatting with the library project manager. A board member was talking intensely to Win Stracke, representative of the Illinois Sesquicentennial Commission, who would give—or, more correctly, sing—the address. Working with the commission, writing the back of the sesquicentennial roadmap, and a brochure of state-wide sesquicentennial activities, Richard Frisbie had learned of Stracke's availability for just this kind of civic observance.

Other board members were taking their chairs. But Mrs. Hendrickson was not ready to ask Mayor John Woods to mark this auspicious occasion with a few words until Carl and Lois Klehm came up the aisle. Waiting, she noted the co-chairpersons of the newly formed Friends of the Library who would be accepting a charter for the organization. She knew that members of the Arlington Heights Woman's Club, always on hand for library celebrations, were upstairs arranging a buffet around a violet (state flower) theme and mentally

179

reviewing statistics about the new facility for the tours they would lead—how many books the high school volunteers had packed and repacked for the move, how many years since Elizabeth Walker had called her friends to the first Chautauqua reading group, how many books were needed to bring the current library up to standard.

She checked the list she'd laid on the podium. She would recognize the woman's club for its gift of a bust of Abraham Lincoln; the friends of Viet Nam war hero Captain Daniel R. Schueren who had donated the podium; the American Legion, the Veterans of Foreign Wars, and the Newcomers Club for donating flags; Arlington Realty, Inc., and the John Hancock Insurance Company for paintings.

She looked down the aisle of chairs set up for the occasion once more. Still no Klehms. She was reminded of the day she'd told the library board that she might be able to get the landscaping donated. Somewhat amazed, they'd expressed a general delight at such a handsome possibility.

Once she had permission, she called Carl Klehm. "May I have five minutes of your time?" She never asked for more. Then she skimmed down in her little car, as she tells it. How well she remembers Carl Klehm coming into his office from the fields, greeting her warmly, and plopping his muddy boots up on his desk. What could he do for her?

Florence Hendrickson appraised her chances of success, hesitant because of the substantial scale of her request. "Well, Carl, I—you know—we need some landscaping at the library and I thought it would be nice if the Klehm name was connected with, uh, the landscaping. In essence," she hurried her words now, "what I am doing is asking for a donation."

Carl Klehm took his feet off the desk and leaned forward. "How much?"

"Well," Florence dropped her voice, "it's not small." She took a deep breath. "It's seven thousand dollars."

Taking the plans she'd brought from the board meeting, the man whose largesse had "greened" the village agreed to donate the entire landscaping to the new library. He ranged the redbuds across the front, covered the mud with sod, moved trees onto the south lawn, protected the much-admired pseudo-copper beech, added ground cover and bushes.

Florence could see the redbuds through the grill above her at this moment. She looked down the aisle one last time and smiled. She could see Carl and Lois. The dedication could begin.

After the guitar-plucking consultant for folk music for the state celebration had cosseted the audience into joining choruses of "Die Gedunkens im Frei," a song for the early German settlers in Arlington Heights; "The House I Live In" to honor the veterans for whom the library was named; a Methodist revival song for the 110-year-old campground in nearby Des Plaines, and his original song of Illinois rivers, and the awards had been made, guests trailed upstairs for tours and refreshments courtesy of the ever-faithful Arlington Heights Woman's Club.

The library was an immediate mecca, and not only for readers. Kids pressed the elevators into continuous service. Their confederates overturned newly planted decorative urns. The parking lot became an instant Indianapolis speedway for bicyclists.

Readers also found their way to Dunton and Euclid. The checkouts jogged from one thousand a day to three thousand, two hundred. By September, 1968, there were 33,520 registered borrowers. The brochure for the dedication had adverted to the crunch expected, pointing out that "finding ways to

181

Opening day inspection by library board president Florence Hendrickson, left, and head librarian Mary Lee Ewalt

make up for the shortage (of volumes) would remain a problem of the library for some time." Beacham said that the book supply was "woefully inadequate."

Win Stracke had told the dedication audience that to his mind, "a library is a great monument to freedom of thought." To realize this ideal, however, there had to be books on the shelves. Nathalie Wallace suggested that the patrons be allowed only three books instead of four. "I can't see why anybody needs to take out four books at one time, anyway," she said.

The library board was offered options. "Would you rather have the books, with a fair increase per capita, with less than total access to them, or would you rather have full access to a full collection with (less than) full service by the staff?" Mrs. Ewalt asked. She explained that presently the patrons were having a hard time finding what they wanted.

"I would have to vote for at least having books on the premises for those who can find them," Frisbie advised.

The library board was wrestling with two problems: increased cost of operation in a building five times as big as the old, and a need to increase rapidly the book collection. Any solution required another referendum.

As if the crunch was not sufficient to keep their attention, the board members began talking about opening the library on Sunday. Bud Beacham, who had a lot of sympathy with commuters, was up for closing on one weekday in order to free staff for Sunday coverage. Frisbie found that solution "utterly unacceptable."

Calling their attention to the "ample room" on the library bookshelves, Beacham brought up the advisability of arranging a dual referendum for 1969 to deal with the operating fund and the purchase of new books. Now that state representative Eugene Schlickman had successfully introduced a bill to change the statute regarding library purchases, libraries throughout the state organized under the Public Library Act of 1965 could bond for expenditures in book acquisition. However, attorney R. Marlin Smith warned the board that the overall bonded indebtedness of the village could not be exceeded so the library board members would have to work closely with the village board.

On a short-term basis, the board voted to ask the North Suburban Library System to support future legislation which would automatically increase the library levy from twelve to fifteen cents per one hundred dollars assessed valuation. An amendment to the Public Library Act was needed for that change.

The two insistent cries that nagged the library board as they met in their new quarters on Dunton Street were not dissimilar to those that had plagued Nellie Best and the woman's club, Nathaniel Moore Banta and the first board, and staff members on Belmont. At long last there was enough room. But there were not enough books by thousands. And there seemed to be no way to control the youngsters who seemed bent on turning the library into the local hangout.

Some of the board members investigated the feasibility of installing closed circuit television in the downstairs foyer and the noisiest corners of the building so that the staff could descry those who disturbed the library peace. Board member Richard Frisbie objected to what he called a watchdog program that smacked of "fascist" tactics. "When I know that I'm being watched on these sets in other buildings, my hackles are raised," he said. Charles Edward saw no difference between the actual presence of a monitor in the area and a set which enabled the monitor to watch student activities.

Mary Lee Ewalt thought of the staff persons who spent their days running up and down stairs, trying to catch young elevator passengers. She reasoned that she'd had more luck asking patrons to quiet down over the intercom than she'd had in person. She nodded when Edward pointed out that the staff were all women who don't "get the respect they deserve."

"You just can't keep up with everything that's happening in the library," he added.

"It's nothing more than what you get when several generations use the same facility," Mary Lee Ewalt said. About the closed circuit monitors, she didn't have feelings one way or the other. The board decided to try the $3,000 to $4,000 system, in spite of Frisbie's continued criticism that the "symbolism isn't right. We have a few young people who are problems, and because of them, we're going to watch all the people."

The second pressing problem was finding the money to buy books, a perennial headache. The board wanted to upgrade the book collection in the next five years to meet standards of the American Library Association which recommended two books per resident. As a matter of interest, Beacham pointed out that North Shore libraries shelved four to six books per person. Estimating that the village population in 1975 would be 78,000, the board wanted to raise the number to 156,000 volumes which meant spending five hundred thousand dollars. The present collection was 65,000—one book per resident.

Before the board could tackle this concern, Mrs. Ewalt suggested a major change in staffing. She wanted to step down as head librarian in favor of Harold J. Ard, then administrator of the Barrington Public Library. "It's nice to have a man around the house," Mary Lee Ewalt suggested as she put forth his name.

Administration on the scale demanded by the new library removed her too far from the "librarian side for her taste," Mrs. Ewalt explained. Besides, the library collection badly needed re-cataloging. She would remain as adult librarian and director of special services, getting that cataloging done.

The board paid tribute to Mary Lee Ewalt, emphasizing that they couldn't stress too strongly that stepping down was "entirely her own idea."

Harold Ard took over on February 1, 1969, as the first professional with a master's degree in library science to serve as chief administrator in Arlington. After terms as materials consultant in the Decatur school system and teacher at Lincoln College, he had been administrator in Barrington, acquiring his degree in library science at Rosary College in River Forest. His announced plan for the Arlington library coincided nicely with Florence Hendrickson's: "to have the greatest library in the state within a few years."

Local historian Daisy Paddock Daniels donates her clipping file to library, Florence Hendrickson, left, and executive librarian Harold Ard

As Florence Hendrickson often said, "A town or a library has no stature if people aren't in back of it. You have to be for Arlington Heights the way Texans are for Texas." She resonated with Harold Ard's forecast.

While Mary Lee Ewalt and her staff cataloged all the new books, and re-cataloged retrospectively as fast as they could, as fast as the need presented itself—without ever collecting a backlog even after the tremendous influx of books that came in 1969—Harold Ard faced the administrative responsibilities that came with increased staff and catapulting usage.

The board congratulated itself—prematurely, as it turned out—that after four score years of cramped quarters they had finally created a structure with enough bookroom to accommodate the projected population of Arlington Heights. Unfortunately, it was bookroom without books.

The Arlington Library had more patrons and fewer books per patron than any neighboring library. Barrington had a ratio of 3.5 books per resident; Mount Prospect, 1.6; Des Plaines, 1.4; Elk Grove Village, 1.5; Palatine, 1.6. The Arlington count was 1.1 per resident. New board president Nathalie Wallace suggested that the goal of two books per capita was the first step toward providing "the ultimate collection."

Now was the appointed time to take advantage of the new state library regulations that Eugene Schlickman had guided through the legislature. About the time the board decided to experiment with the closed circuit disciplinary monitors, they also set a date for a May 17 two-pronged referendum, justifying any voter confusion by the efficiency of passing both referenda simultaneously. Board members explained to the voters that the bond issue would spread the cost of new books over a number of years so that future residents would get to pay for some of the books they took out of the library.

There were two votes, one for the five hundred thousand dollar bond issue, the other for an increase in the board's tax ceiling from twelve to twenty cents per one hundred dollars of assessed valuation. The increase in the taxes for a thirty thousand dollar home would be $1.65 the first year, $6.24 by 1973 when the bond money would be used up, and $11.14 over the current rates by 1979. Beacham noted that this funding would only be appropriate in a community growing as fast as Arlington Heights. In the ten months since the library's opening circulation had jumped thirty-nine percent and registrations nineteen percent. Those card-holders wanted books. They were willing to pay for them. The referenda passed by two to one: 1,017 to 514 for the bond issue and 954 to 576 for the tax ceiling raise.

Once the bonds were sold, 100,600 books could be bought. Rising interest rates made selling the bonds immediately problematical. But Fritz Wolf, president of the Bank and Trust of Arlington Heights, took $145,000 of the bonds, purely to show public spirit because the maximum rate of five percent was not currently favorable on the market. "Their interest is to help the library out of a problem," Beacham announced. Wolf added, "We feel we should participate in community events."

The bank's purchase of the bonds made it possible for the library to purchase a sixty-five-page book order.

Another windfall for the book budget was the $175,000 of the money left over from construction that attorney Smith agreed could be used for book purchases without breaking the law. Ard included a microfilm collection of newspapers in that order.

Meanwhile, back at the building awarded the 1969 Distinguished Building Award by the Chicago chapter of the American Institute of Architects and by the Chicago Association of Commerce and Industry, a "poolroom" atmosphere was spreading. Patrons were snuffing out their cigarettes in the spanking carpeting; one junior high youngster ground his lighted cigar into the floor covering.

The board had had long discussions about smoking before the library opened. Bud Beacham was in favor, as a smoker. Mary Lee Ewalt, also a smoker, befriended the idea because she quickly tired of "don'ts" and "you can'ts." Theoretically, the air conditioning system would remove the smoke so that the privilege for some would not be plague for others.

But the public was not cooperative or neat about their smoking. They didn't use the ashtrays. A high school student complained to the board that junior high students were using the library as a smoking parlor. The carpet soon showed twenty large holes and one hundred small confirmations of careless smokers. What frightened the staff more was the rowdiness. Harold Ard said that "kids were throwing books at each other and verbally assaulting the library staff."

Staff members hesitated to evict the hooligans because "we were afraid they might wait outside the door for us after the building was closed." The chief of police thought smoking was the base of the behavior problem so Harold Ard put up *No Smoking* signs.

As he admits, that was one of his "first controversial acts. Unfortunately, the local newspaper made the announcement before it was officially approved by the library board."

Ard may have been slightly hasty in his ukase against smoking. However, the atmosphere changed immediately for the better, according to a staff member. "It's a pleasure to work there now," Marge Larsen told the newspaper. "We aren't under a strain anymore."

Smoking would not be reinstated.

20.
Joining The System

"Booksellers are generous liberal-minded men," Samuel Johnson wrote in 1756. Book-lenders—men and women—bear out Johnson's aphorism into the twentieth century. At the Arlington Heights Memorial Library a generous book-lending spirit persisted as the library grew. It was an accessible, hospitable, convivial gathering place.

Like Mary Lee Ewalt who allowed smoking at the outset because she was weary of constant prohibitions about the use

of public space, Harold Ard cherished an open-handed tolerance toward patrons' idiosyncracies.

Soon after Palatine artist Harold Kerr's metal sculpture of youngsters reading in a tree was installed under the stairs near the parking lot entrance, Ard got an SOS from the front desk about "unsavory characters" settled under the filigree of twining metal branches.

He scurried down the stairs, determined to preserve the peace—and the piece.

What he found were two teen-agers sitting on the floor under the sculpture eating popcorn. Ard had every intention of marching them out as he enunciated the library rules against food or beverage.

But he couldn't shatter the charming scene. The *bons vivants* were too enthusiastic about their situation. "They said it was the grandest thing since they had a picnic under the Picasso sculpture in the Civic Center Plaza in Chicago last summer," Ard told the paper.

After that disarming confidence, there was no action Ard could bring himself to take. He later confessed that he "didn't have the heart to tell them that they couldn't eat popcorn in the library."

But when it came to lending books (which Arlington taxpayers had voted a bond issue to pay for) to any reader in northern Illinois, the library board of directors found it hard to be "generous book-lenders." In May, 1968, the Arlington library had only had 1.1 books for every resident, scarcely a princely supply. With the bond issue and the funds left over from construction, the library had half again as many books a year later. Those new books were tugging neighboring readers toward summer evening drives to cast their eyes over the recent acquisitions—and then, incredibly, to take them out.

Almost from the beginning, there had been readers outside

the village limits who paid first fifty cents a year, then a dollar, and in time five dollars, to borrow the books that Arlington taxpayers had bought. In 1970 there were fifteen hundred families paying twenty dollars a year for this privilege.

Now the North Suburban Library System, which the library board had voted to join under duress when it became clear that they would not get federal funds for their building unless they cooperated with the state plan, issued a new ultimatum. Every library in the system was asked to institute reciprocal borrowing by July 1, 1971. This meant that a cardholder in any of the thirty-one public libraries in the system could take books out of any of the thirty-one libraries.

Librarians in the system thought that free use of all libraries by all persons in the system was a Utopian idea. An Arlington Heights library card would be useful from Barrington to Evanston and to the state line on the north.

The Arlington library board of directors, however, were not easily convinced that reciprocal borrowing was practical for a library like Arlington's that had a superior, rapidly growing collection.

Ard was blunt. "In theory, I think reciprocal borrowing is great, but to be in favor of it, I think it should be borrowing among equals." That would not be the case locally. Arlington Heights now had a collection of more than 122,000 items; Rolling Meadows, 23,000; Mount Prospect, 58,600, and Des Plaines, about 90,000.

The Arlington library was leery of joining the borrowing system for fear that it might be easier to get into the system than to get out. The board was vigilant about its autonomy even though the NSLS director, Robert R. McClarren, insisted that state legislators would oppose any "state control of libraries just as (they) would with park districts or school districts."

When NSLS was formed after the State of Illinois passed the Library Systems Act in 1966, a plan to provide "free use of the total library resources within the system for all residents holding library cards of any participating library in the area served" was integral to the proposal. That "free use" was reciprocal borrowing. It was meant to be in place by the fifth year of the system's operation.

There had been a reciprocal borrowing pilot program, but none of the big libraries—Evanston, Skokie, Park Ridge, Des Plaines, Mount Prospect, Arlington Heights—had joined. They all feared a drain on their collections.

Bob McClarren was sympathetic to the Arlington position, admitting that the Arlington library was in a unique position, "a strong library surrounded by many smaller libraries." However, he assured the board of directors that there was some quid pro quo. Arlington card-holders were using other system programs. Arlington was the second heaviest user of interlibrary loans, showing Arlington card-holders were using other neighboring book collections. Arlington patrons were also the fifth heaviest users of the system's centralized serial service and the heaviest users of the system's film collection.

During the lengthy, involved discussions that seemed to drag on indefinitely, the library board admitted that they were not necessarily opposed to the theory of reciprocal borrowing but "felt that the library should be reimbursed for the number of books that leave the library when Arlington Heights residents do not borrow the same number of books from other libraries" (as card-holders from neighboring libraries borrowed at Arlington).

On March 21, 1971, when Richard Frisbie moved that the board participate in reciprocal borrowing, provided that details of the plan were acceptable, only he and Charles Edward voted aye. The board was willing to endorse the plan only for a later date when neighboring libraries had grown.

This was an issue on which board members got input from their public. Residents chewed over reciprocal borrowing as they chewed hamburgers at summer barbecues. They stopped board members on the trains to Chicago to object to letting "their" books out of town. An Arlington resident held up Richard Frisbie in One Illinois Center in Chicago until he could register his complaint.

There was room for debate. A Mount Prospect village trustee was widely quoted as asking why that village's residents should pay for a lot of books "when our people can go to Arlington Heights?" On the other hand, Rolling Meadows authorities wanted Arlington restrictions to put the heat on Rolling Meadows taxpayers to vote funds.

According to Frisbie, the Arlington library directors were ahead of the residents in the liberality of their policy. "Being on a board educates the members to the realities, widens their view. The process of making responsible decisions for the community has a liberalizing influence."

That liberalization waxed slowly. In October, 1969, the board had refused to be part of the NSLS experimental program. At that time both Ard and the board were against participating. There was even talk of retiring from NSLS if reciprocal borrowing was demanded. Meanwhile reciprocal borrowing was shedding its threatening character.

The first two hundred readers who used it liked it. "Most of these borrowers are people who use the library regularly for doing research," McClarren noted. Besides, NSLS distributed largesse. Under the coordinated acquisitions program the Arlington library was receiving thirty thousand dollars for a collection of books on education which would be housed at Arlington and available to everyone in the system. The local staff could pick the books on child psychology, history of education, and parent help they thought suitable.

Now when the board talked about leaving NSLS, Ard could say, "But we'll lose the collection." Board member Roland Ley still countered with the argument that "it seems ridiculous that the Arlington Heights taxpayers should share the facilities they paid for with everyone without any incentive for other libraries to build up their collections."

It wasn't that the board didn't see the desirability of having all the information in the country available at the Dunton Avenue library at some future date. A systems person from New York, playing on that aspiration, told a local audience that "we are all looking for the Nirvanah when we are all plugged into a huge data bank and can push a button and have everything from the Library of Congress in our local libraries." He warned his listeners that this would never happen "unless we take the first steps." By December, 1971, only Elgin and Arlington Heights were holding out on the first step toward this encompassing eventuality.

Admitting that the original reciprocal borrowing agreement had looked "very bad," Frisbie told the board in January, 1972, that the system had agreed to the two main concessions the Arlington board wanted. The library would receive fifty cents per unit for materials borrowed from it in excess of materials that Arlington patrons borrowed from other libraries. Also, the library had a document stating that if reciprocal borrowing was detrimental the library could drop out. Frisbie once again moved that the board adopt reciprocal borrowing. Board member Roland Ley noted that the board's reciprocal borrowing committee hadn't reported yet. Ley saw the possible loss of a $3,244 federal grant for library books "as another pressure tactic. The grant should not have any

195

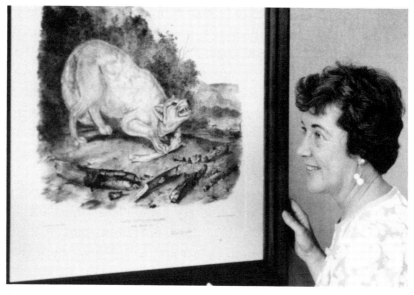

Library board president Nathalie Wallace with donated Audubon print

bearing on our decision on the important issue of reciprocal borrowing." Again the motion was defeated.

At the end of the month what board president Nathalie Wallace called "another twist by NSLS to force us to join the system's reciprocal borrowing program" developed. Arlington Heights could not have reciprocal borrowing with Chicago unless it joined the local reciprocal borrowing system.

When the approval for reciprocal borrowing finally came in March, 1972, by a vote of five to two, the ratification was grudging. The Arlington board got everything it asked: the federal grant, compensation for excess borrowing, permission to withdraw at any time. But reciprocal borrowing committee chairman Robert Melroy announced that he would be the first to recommend withdrawing from the system if it adversely affected Arlington Heights library patrons.

196

Nathalie Wallace was equally restrained in her endorsement. "I think we are just tired of being punched at by NSLS," she said, "and now have taken the attitude of giving it a try."

As it worked out, no more than two percent of the items checked out of the Arlington library that April, 1972, were borrowed by patrons living outside the village. Of the 69,623 items borrowed from the library that month only 1,246 were borrowed by non-residents. In that same month 74 Arlington Heights library patrons borrowed materials from other libraries in the system.

"We don't feel the amount of borrowing from non-Arlington Heights patrons is excessive," Harold Ard told the newspaper.

Through all this hassle the board was experimenting with other varieties of largesse. The library bought Talking Machines to read books to disabled patrons. They worked rather like record players. For the Talking Machines there were Talking Books. Here again the interlibrary cooperation was a blessing, widening the range of Talking Books available to every disabled patron.

For those who had trouble reading the fine print in ordinary books but who were not candidates for Talking Machines, the library added a wide range of large-print books with type three times the standard size. The collection included a large-print encyclopedia. Anyone who wanted to read a book unavailable in large-print could use one of the five print magnifiers on stands.

In addition to the Talking Machines, the library added Rolling Wheels. Once the library had been a comfortable walking distance for anyone who hiked into the middle of town. With village boundaries stretching toward the toll road on the south and the county line on the north, trips to the library were an expedition for those at the greatest remove. To bring the library to those who couldn't easily bring themselves to the library, the board splurged on a used 1966 bookmobile from the St. Lurie-Okeechobee Regional Library at Fort Pierce, Florida. The conception was extravagant in a way, but the vehicle itself was a bargain. It would bring the library to patrons at local parks, schools, and nursing homes.

That kind of expansion was expected. Technical aids for the handicapped. A Parnassus on wheels. But running the building further down Dunton Avenue? That was the limit. It was only four years since a library had been thrust up on Dunton to serve a population of 80,000. There weren't 80,000 people in Arlington Heights.

Board members realized this, but they also knew there was no room on the shelves for all the books the library was buying—more than any other library in the state except Chicago. There wasn't enough seating for patrons on some evenings and Sunday afternoons—already one of the most popular library days of the week. "I never go near the library on Sunday," patrons who had that option admitted. The audio-visual department was near capacity. "Our architect said we shouldn't add any more shelving, we've added more than he wanted to see already," Harold Ard commented.

Expansion talk went on hold for a time when executive librarian Harold Ard announced that he was moving into a new position as head of the municipal library of Jackson, Mississippi, with a central library and five branches. Ard left Arlington Heights with the gratitude of the board and a good feeling about the work he'd done. Consultant Guenter A. Jansen, director of the Suffolk Cooperative Library System in New York, assessed Arlington's collection as excellent, thoughtfully built, and well maintained. "You are to be congratulated on the development of a truly fine library, which shows evidence of careful spending," he told Ard and the staff.

Ard noted other advancements during his tenure:

Mechanical completion of new building, purchasing of books and equipment

Passage of a successful double referendum to buy books and raise tax rate

Doubling of book collection to present 141,500 total

Establishment of largest audio-vidual department in state

Establishment of successful book processing center

Cooperation with North Suburban Library System with reciprocal borrowing and coordinated acquisition

Increase in number and quality of staff

When Harold Ard left in October, 1972, and Mary Lee Ewalt moved into the interim head librarian spot until his replacement was recruited, it seemed that the issue of reciprocal borrowing which had dominated much of Ard's regime was finally accepted and implemented.

But the issue was not comfortably laid to rest. Whenever there was an election there was sure to be someone—"usually a non-reader," a candidate observed—who lofted the reciprocal borrowing ball into the game plan. "It's a sore issue with a lot of people because they don't know the benefits we get from the exchange."

Fourteen years after its ratification in March, 1972, a library board president was asked whether the issue of reciprocal borrowing was settled once and for all. She didn't think so. "I don't think that reciprocal borrowing in this town will ever be over with," Jan Tucker said.

21.
Expansion On Dunton Street

"If I have done nothing else for the people of Arlington Heights, I have given them Frank Dempsey." Richard Frisbie was chairperson of the search committee to find a new executive librarian when Harold Ard decided to trade northern winters for the balmy leniency of Mississippi seasons.

This was really the first time that the Library Board of Directors was responsible for finding an executive to run the library. In the early days the job had been passed on casually. "Do you know anyone who wants to be head librarian here?" Evelyn Stadelman had asked the women at the front desk. When Mary Lee Ewalt stepped down, she had already spotted Harold Ard as a capable and qualified successor.

By 1972 the board had a library building accorded a Distinguished Building Award by the American Institute of Architects, an increasingly competent staff, and a community ready to support any reasonable recommendations. What they needed was an executive to use all these gains to the greatest advantage of the library's patrons.

As search committee chairperson, Frisbie advertised in the appropriate journals and turned up fifty candidates. Some of the candidates simply did not have the requisite experience. Frisbie organized a series of interviews at his Chicago office on Michigan Avenue for all of those who qualified, on a two-an-afternoon basis.

When he had whittled the slate down to the top three candidates, he invited them to meet the search committee, and then the full board. At a special meeting on January 16, 1973, the board agreed that its choice for executive librarian was the former librarian at Berkeley, California. Frisbie moved to employ Frank Dempsey. The vote was unanimous. Frank Dempsey would be invited to trade the balmy leniency of California seasons for the rigorous winters of the Middle West.

To the whole board Frank Dempsey was the overwhelmingly fit choice. He had inaugurated a great many changes and innovations at Berkeley that the board hoped he could replicate in Arlington Heights. Dempsey had told the search committee, and then the total board, that in 1959-60 the Berkeley library circulated 656,627 items. In 1970-71—eight years after his accession at the Berkeley library—the total was over a million, and for the fourth straight year the Berkeley Public Library was first in the state in terms of per capita circulation for cities of 100,000 and over.

**Executive Librarian
Frank Dempsey**

DAILY HERALD PHOTO

Some of Dempsey's innovations had drawn nation-wide interest. When the San Francisco Foundation gave the library a grant for a bookmobile, its concept as a "Media Machine" was novel enough to attract the attention of *Newsweek*. The Arlington board expressed equal interest in Berkeley's reciprocal borrowing program (always a hot topic in Arlington Heights), its after-hours telephone referral service and, particularly, Dempsey's work with local, state, and national Friends of the Library groups.

Having "found" Frank Dempsey for the people of Arlington Heights, Frisbie received his due. He was elected president of the Library Board of Directors, May 8, 1973, following Nathalie Wallace, one of the distinguished line of woman's club members who had served the library over the years, never "weary in well-doing."

Like Nathaniel Moore Banta and John Beaty who had served on the first library board set up in Arlington Heights,

Library board president
Richard Frisbie

202

Frisbie was a writer. While serving on the library board—although not during his presidency—Frisbie was elected president of the Society of Midland Authors, an organization formed in 1915 by a group of authors that included Hamlin Garland, Harriet Monroe, and Vachel Lindsay.

With a new librarian at the helm, Frisbie and the other board members could go back to dickering on the placement of a needed library addition. Should it top the present building? That idea was pretty much zapped by a predecessor board that had "saved" $60,000 by not paying for a sturdy enough base for upward mobility. Should the addition stretch out over the parking lot?

Should the expansion come from enclosing the space under the current upper level? By July, 1973, the head of the building committee, Lawrence Dickerson, had met with architects Robert Chaney and Milo Vanek who told him that a feasibility study would take about a month and cost about three thousand, five hundred dollars.

The need was obvious. In 1972 the circulation was 800,000, more than ten books per patron. Frank Dempsey pointed out that the library had to continue to buy new books—eighty percent of all circulation on any given day was new material—but there was no place on the shelves to squeeze in new acquisitions.

Even though the library now housed 150,000 volumes, with more than 430 serials (magazines and newspapers), it was still falling short of the American Library Association quota of 3.5 books per capita. That would mean 245,000 books. "It's a standard we would like to meet, but at the present time, even if through miraculous circumstances we should have the 93,000 needed, we would have no place to put them."

Dempsey could see that those places for books would have

to be created. Already the Arlington library ranked third among the 258 public libraries in Illinois in circulation of library materials. The Chicago Public Library and the Rockford Public Library were first and second.

Arlington circulated 859,831 items—enough books that, laid end to end, would have stretched from Dunton and Euclid twelve miles east and north to Highland Park.

That usage is an "indication of the extent to which Arlington Heights people use and appreciate their library," Dempsey said.

All those users got a Christmas present from the library board that December, 1973. The library which had been raised to serve 80,000 residents was now going to be inflated by 25,000 square feet, room for the 95,000 additional books the ALA thought appropriate. Browsers and students would have 169 more seats. The Dunton Room seating would go up from the present 90 to 140.

"It seems that Arlington Heights people use (a library) a lot more than normal," architect Robert Chaney commented.

If the board meant to build out west over the parking lot, Chaney suggested that this time the board should spend the additional thirty thousand dollars to construct a roof on which a second floor could be added at a later date. Actually, there were two plans on the docket: (1) for a separate building with a mall and passageway between it and the library, and (2) a physical extension of the present building.

Leaning to plan two, Robert Melroy suggested at the October board meeting that the library board ask the village for the land south of the library building.

That parcel was presently a village parking lot. On the Dunton Street side, however, there loomed a large sign reminding passersby that the block bounded by Vail, Fremont, Dunton, and St. James was the SITE OF THE FUTURE

CULTURAL CENTER. For years the Cultural Commission, headed in 1974 by Sidney Rosenfeld, had been planning a convertible auditorium seating four to five hundred persons for community theater productions which could be modified into a sixteen-hundred-seat concert hall.

There was no question about the enthusiasm of the hard-working proponents nor of the Arlington Heights Arts Council, an umbrella group of local theater and music groups, for the project. The arts council had donated $8,000 toward a fee for architects' plans. Business leaders donated $3,000. When the Cultural Commission couldn't raise the $25,000 needed for the initial study, however, the members were not sanguine about collecting the $3,000,000 required to build the cultural center their sign so poignantly advertised.

Rosenberg suggested regretfully that he had a "strong feeling that when we report the lack of progress we have made, the trustees won't just let us sit on the land if other people need it." He didn't feel the commission should stymie the library's plans.

When library board president Richard Frisbie first went to the village board with his slides showing "the crowd, the buzz, the murmurings of this great hive," the library, he pointed out firmly that "we don't have room in the library for the books we need."

Village trustees interviewed both the library board representatives and the cultural center commissioners. Sensing that the cultural center was a long shot, Frisbie assured the village board that the library board would be very receptive "to working with the (Cultural) Commission to build many cultural aspects of this plan." He couldn't tell at that point how much of a drag the Cultural Commission proposal would be to library plans.

Rosenfeld, to seize what remnants of the Cultural Commission plan could be salvaged, agreed that if his commission had exhausted its credibility, it could "at least go into a clinch."

At first village finance committee member Frank Palmatier speculated that the village should sell the property to the library, saving the money for the Cultural Commission to build at a later date. The money the village used to buy the property had come from funds donated by developers for public land purposes.

However, the village attorney considered the library's need for expansion uniquely attributable to the growth of the village. This persuaded Frank Palmatier and other village trustees that the library should have free use of the property to its south. The library board would have to go to the public for a referendum on bonds to build the projected addition.

There were advantages to the location on the south over throwing a second floor over the parking lot: (1) the continuation of library services during construction, (2) the economical extension of the present heating and cooling systems, and (3) the attractive look of a unified building.

The library board worked out a three-phase plan with architects Robert Chaney and Milo Vanek to take to the voters. Phase one would take care of the immediate need for space; phase two would provide for future expansion; phase three would provide a five hundred-seat lecture hall/theater which would be connected to the library by a corridor and exhibition gallery.

The board took their plan to the voters at the April 1, 1975 election. Voters turned it down. The public hadn't supported an independent cultural center. Nor would they pay for a cultural center in the library.

Books, yes. More taxes, no. Cultural center, no. The voters nixed the addition, nor did they support a raise in the authorized tax rate to forty cents on each one hundred dollars evaluation of their homes. But they did vote for book bonds. Ironically, the public could not have the bond issue for more books unless they also approved an extension of the building because that was the way the law was written when Bud Beacham had gone to Representative Eugene Schlickman over a decade before.

The referendum had failed.

The library board would have to go back to the public once more. What board members realized after they lost the referendum was that they had thought of the cultural-center-in-the-library as the project of the village and the Cultural Commission. The board, on taking stock of the referenda, could see that it wasn't enough to have those entities out hustling for the library addition. The library board would have to do a better job of organizing and selling its story to the public.

It was not an easy task. The economy was depressed, the economic picture unsteady. Voters were resisting new taxes, suggesting that, "You should make do with what you have." One patron recommended creating the needed space by eliminating tables and chairs in the children's area, "the excess of display cases," the rack displaying current magazines. "The large carpeted, tiered seating area where, I imagine, a story lady reads to preschoolers is delightful, but how necessary?"

Frank Dempsey repeated the historical fact that "in times of recession and depression, library usage goes up. People don't have money to buy their own books so they borrow from the library. They don't have money for trips, plays, and concerts so they read more."

He added, explaining the vote loss, "I guess you might say that books have positive vibes but taxes don't."

Frisbie saw the vote loss as a misunderstanding. He commented that "voters obviously didn't grasp the whole situation if they pass a book bond (issue) and don't provide space to put the books in. It doesn't add up."

He theorized that the voters, by voting for one part of the referendum, were telling the board that they were asking too much. He suggested going back to the voters with a smaller package. Joyce Zeller who'd served as chairperson for the citizens' committee that had worked vigorously for the referendum considered this attitude a failure of nerve. "Either you need it or you don't," she said. "If you don't, then you had no right asking for it in the first place."

When the library board fixed on February 28, 1976, for a second referendum, they pitched out the theater, cutting the $591,000 it would have cost. They substituted a 300-person meeting area with a stage and film projection room, but not the sloping floor that would have made it appropriate for dramatic productions. An additional meeting room was essential, however. "The Dunton Room is just being trampled," Frisbie said. "We have a need for one right now."

This time when the pro-referendum advocates went to neighborhood associations and organization meetings, they didn't have to compete with other candidates, they had time to answer questions, and they found an "overwhelmingly positive response," according to Frank Dempsey. The ad hoc group, SHELF (Subcommittee to Help Expand Library Facilities) conducted what Dempsey called "their great phone calling effort," as well as a series of appearances and slide shows at homeowners' groups, clubs, and civic organizations.

This dedication was rewarded—though not by the margin the library board members would have liked. On February 28, a bond issue to meet the library's needs for five to ten years was carried by a vote of 2,201 to 1,881. The people in three precincts voted firmly against the expansion.

The next month the Arlington library, according to the careful notes that administrative aide Jo Running took at the board meetings, circulated more items than in any month in its history—94,392 books, magazines, and records. That nine percent increase over March, 1975, was "phenomenal," Frank Dempsey said.

What was also phenomenal, but not a matter of rejoicing, was the number of books leaving the library under the jackets of the patrons, instead of under their arms. An inventory in June, 1975, showed that nine percent of the total reference collection was missing. In some subject areas fourteen percent of the books were missing. Overall, the loss was eleven to twelve percent in non-fiction. A 1974 inventory showed that eighteen percent of the books purchased during a seven-year period couldn't be found. The highest losses were in books on car repairs, mentally handicapped children, photography, and witchcraft.

In 1975—a recession year—most of the pilfered stock was books on real estate, business, and various kinds of reference. Board president Frisbie couldn't understand the mechanism. "Why do people steal from the public library when they can have the books for free? The stupidity of it is almost beyond belief," he noted.

Just as a policeman stalking the library gun in holster seemed an unfortunate symbol to early board members, so the present members of the board resisted a barrier at the front door to stop people who couldn't stop themselves from cadging a cookbook or two. However, the loss of eighteen percent of the newest books convinced them of the need for restraints.

The board agreed to pay $13,985—money that could have been used to buy books—to install a turnstile at the door which would set off an alarm when a patron tried to slip contraband past the Checkpoint theft prevention system.

"We all feel very badly this had to happen, but that's the way it has to be," a library employee commented. Both staff and board were dealing with the realities of their uncommon achievement. The ninth biggest city in the state had the third largest book collection. This meant that the protection of the collection had to be as sophisticated as its accumulation.

Building a library to hold that collection in 1975, the board did not assume, as boards had in 1950 and 1965, that they were building the town's ultimate library. They simply stated that doubling the library's size should satisfy demand for five to ten years.

As it turned out, they were right on target.

22.
Friends Of The Library

When the library board lost its referendum in 1975, the directors looked around for reenforcements before they tried again. The next time they marshalled their arguments for a needed expansion—at least one they saw as needed—they wanted a cadre of informed, committed library users behind them.

They wanted friends.

They wanted Friends of the Library. There had been a vigorous, enterprising Friends of the Library group when everyone in town was energized by the beckoning potential of the new library on Dunton. As early as February, 1968, Harold Ard had directed a steering committee headed by civic activist Mary Schlott and Robert Staley, chairperson of the English department at Forest View High School, to organize a Friends group. When the library was dedicated in June, 1968, the Friends of the Library were right up front to receive their local charter during the ceremonies.

Designated an Illinois non-profit corporation to which contributions were tax-deductible, the Friends were a service group dedicated to encouraging the public to use the library. "Most of us worked hard to help pass the referendum that made the new library possible," one of the members said. "Now we are looking forward to providing the kinds of programs and services that will make the library better used."

They were very energetic. They organized summer reading hours for the youngsters, and as a charming fillip, they set up programs that fall for the mothers who brought their children to story hours. If the children were going to be entertained—and taught something—so were their mothers. "Why should mothers just sit around and wait?" Friends asked themselves—and provided parents with concerts by the Countryside Chamber Ensemble and a series of informative lectures by local experts. It was Janice Jenkins' idea of a "mother's escape plan," good coffee and good talk generated by a speaker who would bring his or her medical, artistic, or current-affairs expertise to the forum.

The Friends organized "an evening with Mark Twain," a slide show by the Boy Scouts, and opportunities for local audiences to meet local authors. "The Northwest suburbs have an unusual number of local authors, especially in the field of non-fiction," the Friends noted. They invited in Richard Dunlop, Bruce Ladd, Frances Altman, Norman Richards, and the library's own Richard Frisbie to talk to relatively small but intensely interested audiences. Having decided that parents ought to be able to see the same films their children routinely watched in Greek civilization and Shakespeare classes, the Friends borrowed enough films from School District 214 to show a series including *The Odyssey* and *Oedipus Rex*. They also had a comedy series.

In the usual course of business transfers and social shifts, the original Friends of the Library lost their momentum and petered out. For some years there was no active group. But there were always library staff and board people who lamented the loss of this quite possibly influential group.

When Frank Dempsey came from Berkeley where he'd operated with Friends groups and when Jan Tucker was elected to the library board, a revival was a likelihood. One of Tucker's concerns from the start was the re-establishment of a Friends group, in conjunction with a volunteer corps. At the time it was board member Tom Dooley who was assigned to run down leads provided by board members to find some enthusiastic library user to re-organize the Friends.

It was not an easy task. Month after month Dooley reported that he'd not been successful—so far—and asked for more leads. Finally, from a notice placed at the circulation desk, enough interested parties were collected in December, 1976, in the Dunton Room to elect one of their members, Barry Demovsky—a resident in the securities business who spent a lot of time at the library encouraging his children to read—as president.

"No one wanted to do it," Demovsky recalls. "Yet we all knew the library needed help." Actually, the possibilities for the Friends were wide open. "I liked taking tours," Demovsky says, "so I started Friends' outings. We went to the symphony and Ravinia. There was a big turnout for the King Tut exhibit at the Field Museum. We made a lot of money from that even though that wasn't our intention." An Egyptologist from the museum, Lee Gibbs, lectured at the library in advance of the tour and then accompanied the group in the tour bus.

Friends invited local people into the library to hear authors Bill Brashler and Arthur Maling. In a stroke of good fortune the year DePaul's basketball team went to number three in the NBA tournament, the Friends had Ray Meyer as their speaker at their annual meeting. True, as the Friends' president said, the audience "was mostly small boys and their fathers." Still, the annual meeting was jammed.

The Friends' first used book sale during Frontier Days netted $243.06, scarcely giving any inkling of the incredible town institution this semi-annual book sale would become.

Books that didn't find a good home at the book sales, donated books, and surplus library books went into a Book

Boutique the Friends set up across from the circulation desk. Patrons could pick up a bestseller of former days for a quarter, or a paperback for a dime.

Library board member Jan Tucker, who saw the library as the "heart of the community," encouraged Friends to be advocates to "stretch the library's resources." As liaison with the Friends, Tucker appreciated their service to the library. "The library gives us so much that I think there are a number of people in the community who'd like to give something in return," she said, inviting an increased membership.

Phyllis Parlee, an early president of the Friends who doubled as book sale chairperson, struck gold when she tried to persuade Margaret Gray to be one of those persons "who'd like to give something in return." To Margaret, "a Gray around books was like Brer Rabbit in the briar patch." Of course she would like to help with the book sales. "But I can't help you this time," she told Parlee. "I'll help the next time."

Book sale

214

In short order, Parlee's invitation was parlayed into Gray's stellar supervision of future sales. Chairperson Gray, often co-chairing with Helen Corwin, went on to average $7,000 a sale spring and fall in the Hendrickson Room. By 1986 it was hard to imagine the book sales without her ringing voice pointing out fine arts titles here, the children's books against the wall, and the records on the stage. Satisfied customers left, hefting big bags of books and big smiles of anticipation.

Gray needed sixty helpers to put out the books, man the cashboxes and clean up afterwards. The rewards were rich for the Friends, for the customers, and for the library community. With the money they gleaned the Friends added cultural amenities to the library that could not appropriately be paid for out of tax money.

The list is endless: the lighted globe, the furniture for the Friends Lounge, the Calder jute wall hanging, a brochure describing the library's art works, a contribution to the fountain (and plants), *The Plan of St. Gall*, turntables, reader printer, a doll case, a Jane Redman weaving, John Kearney's

Friends Foyer, gift of Friends of the Library

ram sculpture, shelving, a compact disc player, the McLean sculpture, a poster machine, a Burlini mobile, a dollar bill changer, a microwave oven for the staff, this book. By the spring of 1986 the Friends had spent $65,606.42 on practical gifts and esthetic enhancement.

The Friends were "the bulwark for us, another voice for us in the community" that Jan Tucker had hoped for during the referendum for the 1978 addition on the library. When the expansion made possible by the referendum was initiated at a ground-breaking in February, 1977, it was the Friends of the Library who sponsored the reception in the Dunton Room. A handful of village officials, government representatives, interested residents, and library board members shivered in the February cold to watch president Richard Frisbie turn over the first shovelful of "suspiciously soft earth" to initiate the expansion of the library from 40,000 square feet to 80,000.

Acknowledging the bitter weather, Dempsey suggested that it would be miraculous "if the shovel rather than the ground is not broken." He wondered what else would break as bulldozers chewed up the heavy clay soil packed down under the parking lot, knowing that there was a "second city of wires, cables, pipes, and conduit" under any suburban street. He knew for sure that there was a 12-inch village water main under Fremont Street which was being vacated for the new library building.

In giving up the cultural center land to the library, village trustee Frank Palmatier suggested that the part of the parking lot which the village was not presently giving up to the library would be kept available "for future possible expansion of the Arlington Heights Memorial Library." He knew that the 1976 board could not bind future boards; he simply wanted "to express the sentiment of this board."

216

Ten years before, Florence Hendrickson had insisted that the library should have windows that did not need drapes, an unnecessary and, to her, unesthetic window accessory. Architect Chaney designed long narrow windows which serendipitously—according to patrons—framed the "copper beech" tree, the Arlington Heights Historical Society building, and the century-old houses at Euclid/Dunton's other three corners. Now these windows became magic casements, opening on the sight of yawning excavations in the earth south of the library.

Children were riveted to the sills, gripped by the spectacle of bulldozers scratching out the enormous hole, power shovels hoisting up the clay, and trucks hauling in the raw materials to double the capacity of the library for those books which English historian Edward Gibbon called "the faithful mirrors that reflect to our mind the minds of sages and heroes."

Emma Wolfinger, who'd made a practice of bringing her granddaughter Elizabeth to the library each time she visited from Woodstock, couldn't tell now which was the greater enticement: "the faithful mirrors" of sages and heroes or the windows on the absorbing world of building and hauling machines. "I couldn't get her away from her front seat at the construction theatricals to pick out books to take home," she recalls.

Another kind of machine was taking over inside the library. On December 8, 1976 the library computer arrived. It was running within the hour. This didn't mean that it could be put to use immediately. That goal was months away. Before the LIB5100 could check out books, staff would have to put zebra labels on library cards and feed into the computer all the information about the library's books. Staff set August 1 as a target date to go on line and proceeded to train the personnel who would be tucking the patrons' selections under the terminals at the circulation check-out desk. Twenty-five to thirty people worked a total of 217 hours a week at three computer terminals to type in all the newly purchased books. By October, 1977, staff had entered 8,000 patrons. They pushed the target date to go on line to December, not wanting to cause delays for the patrons at the check-out desk. By that time they hoped to have 190,000 items and 40,000 patrons entered. But by December only sixty-five percent of the item total and thirty-five percent of the patron total was in the computer.

It was March 2, 1978, before the library could celebrate Z (for Zebra) Day when the computerized circulation system went into operation. Light pens were used to scan and record the Zebra labels which the staff had been attaching to the book collection for over a year. The new head of the library's circulation department touted the system's big advantages. According to Richard Hanrath, the computer "has made our reserve system and sending out overdue notices more efficient.

"With the new system, we can tell if a given book is on the shelf or not," Hanrath explained. "Another big improvement is in handling lost library cards. When a patron notifies us his card is lost, he is issued a new one and we feed the information into the computer which then will not accept the lost card if someone else tries to use it."

Challenging as the transition to computers at the circulation desk was, the bother couldn't compare with the move into the library addition that summer. Patrons were told the library would be closed for a month and that they should make use of neighboring libraries for the interim as neighboring card-holders had been using the Arlington library for years. They were not pleased. A patron asked in *The Penny Saver* if dismantling the shelves and laying the carpet "cost the taxpayers additional money over the original pretty expensive cost? How could they plan that without knowing exactly how long it would take? And what did the library staff do all month when the library was closed?"

The ever-ebullient executive librarian pleaded Dempsey's Law, (a corollary of Murphy's Law that if anything can go wrong it will): EVERYTHING TAKES LONGER. "Multiply the time you have been promised to finish any project by its own square root and you might get a realistic completion date. Rome wasn't built in a day," he wrote in *Read Out,* "because the day it was supposed to happen nobody showed up."

In a more serious response, he called the expansion "a gargantuan operation," adding that it would "be impossible to provide any kind of meaningful service during this once-in-a-lifetime move."

The library was late in opening, he explained, because "the new shelving we needed to put books on didn't arrive when promised; the carpet people (through no fault of ours) got behind schedule, and totally unforeseen electrical power failures threw our entire timetable out of whack." He assured the letter-writer that there was plenty for the staff to do. For one thing, there were still thousands of books to receive zebra labels and to be fed into the computer.

Not only books had to be moved from one station to another but all the collateral materials: reader printers; cassette players; photocopy machines (color and black); movie projectors for home use; the audio/visual materials including phonograph records, musical scores, framed art prints, microforms, sculptures, and sheet music. The library housed over 225,000 books, 500 periodicals, and 41 newspaper subscriptions, with three particularly strong subject collections in law, education, and health sciences.

219

By the time the addition was ready for dedication, the library board had decided that the handsome, 265-seat community room should honor Florence Hendrickson "who served with inspiration as president of our library board," as Frank Dempsey put it. "The people of Arlington Heights are indebted to her for providing the leadership which in many ways was responsible for the fine library service we have today."

To the Florence J. Hendrickson Room, then, came the library board, their honored guest, Mrs. Hendrickson, and many library well-wishers to hear poet-in-residence John Dickson read his dedicatory poem, *The Cornerstone.* The Arlington Heights Garden Club made big, beautiful bouquets for the occasion; the Music for Youth String Quartet played Mozart.

The new library was double the size of the old. The first day it was opened the circulation was double the usual total. At the end of the year it was announced that the Arlington Heights Memorial Library was the single busiest facility of its kind in the state of Illinois. More books were borrowed from the Arlington library than from any other public library building in the state, including the main library and cultural center on Michigan Avenue (combined) in Chicago.

The gargantuan operation was a gargantuan success.

23.
Hard Questions

Lois Davidheiser doesn't charge into new decisions and situations. Her husband teases her: "If the pioneers had waited for you, they would never have crossed the Appalachians." An appreciative board member who served when Davidheiser was elected president of the board in May, 1981, puts her habit of forethought and discretion a little differently: "Lois has an excellent mind, and she always asks the hard questions. Every board needs a person like her."

A business major at the University of Delaware (whose counselor advised her that women "didn't go into accounting"), Davidheiser knew the library first from the circulation

**Library board president
Lois Davidheiser**

DAILY HERALD PHOTO

desk, as clerk and soon as assistant head of circulation. Bringing that insider's experience to the board deliberations gave her a natural insight into matters of personnel, in particular. Her business background tilted her interest both to the advanced technology possible in the library and the balance needed between the cost of that technology and the advisability of keeping "the tax rate at the point where it is now."

She wanted patrons to get good value.

"The board feels its primary responsibility is to be honest with the public about library issues and needs," Davidheiser says. Her major concern was seeing that "the average patron can find what he or she needs at the library."

More and more in the early eighties that meant having the technology to give the patron what s/he wanted. Even in the community services department supervised by Carol Rickert, the library needed technology, in this case a new, larger bookmobile, to bring items to local nursing homes, schools, parks, and homebound patrons. Technology included audio-visual devices, talking machines, and reader magnifiers. Anyone who was homebound and loved to read could get regular service. "We have prepared a check-list of various categories of books, which we bring to the homebound person, and make monthly deliveries and pick-ups at the patrons' convenience. Records, cassettes, films, and other audio-visual materials are available for them," Rickert told *Read Out.*

But the super technology for the library (which Davidheiser characterizes as "a super place") was the large-capacity computer from Computer Library Systems, Inc., which was housed in a "trouble-free" environment in the spring of 1982.

The data base on the original computer was almost full. The library needed an increased capacity. Having had some experience with "downtime" and the laborious nuisance of recording book transactions by hand, staff and board agreed that the CSLI computer should have a room of its own (not a spot in the basement like the first computer) which would have the necessary climate controls to soothe the computer's psyche. Its compressor was to have a chain link fence and a protective cage on the southwest corner of the library building.

CSLI was providing preventive maintenance for the computer on a regular basis and the record for uptime on the new computer was remarkably good. Each morning at 7 a.m. one of the three computer operators came in to copy a set of back-up discs with the information from the day before. The computer then printed out a daily log, containing the circulation statistics for the previous day. It also printed overdue and fine notices which had once been written laboriously by hand.

The rest of the time operators entered bibliographic data for new materials, including Dewey number, author, title, publisher for new books. This computer could handle three times as much information as the old. More, it was geared to participate in the intrasystem computerized resource sharing project of the North Suburban Library System which allowed each participating library to search other member libraries' data bases for specific books. It could even place reserves on them.

In a short while the computer was able to search for materials by subject as well as title. That hadn't been possible until now.

The changeover to the new computer went smoothly except for what was called a "head crash," in the new parlance. Two days of records were lost.

The uptime generally was excellent, ninety-four percent

from March 6 to April 8. There was a good deal of equipment involved. Circulation had four laser scanners, one light pen and four CRTs which made check-in and check-out much faster than they had been in the history of the library. There were also two terminals in youth services which gave access to that entire department.

Reference had two CRTs, one with a swivel base. One CRT was kept in the adult services office where it soon paid off in terms of work flow. Audio-visual had a laser scanner and a CRT which enabled the staff to handle transactions on the spot and to place reserves instantly. Community services, with one CRT, could check main library materials in and out.

Computers, "something new from the sky" like Dr. Seuss's *oobleck,* were "falling" everywhere into the library. But not without fallout. A patron opened the top of the adult microcomputer and pulled out an eighty-column card while the machine was on. The memory chips inside blew up. Compushop in Buffalo Grove repaired the damage without charge but from then on a protective shield was kept over the unit.

The youth services department made an Apple II computer available to young people, including the software to go with it. Always good at geography, executive librarian Frank Dempsey popped in a diskette on "State Capitals." When he got all the answers correct, the computer patted him on the head, figuratively, with a "Good for you, Frank, you got them all right."

Dempsey confessed in his *Read Out* column that he had never been on a first-name basis with a machine before. "It was a sobering experience."

By November, 1982, there were three microcomputers available at the library which could be reserved by the public and used without charge. The library bought software, some for work, some for play. There were also computer manuals, books, and handbooks to help people work the new technology. The staff could provide guidance and assistance but not in-depth instruction.

What was exciting about the computers was their incredible ability to reach into other systems and pluck out esoteric information that patrons couldn't put their fingers on locally. Seventeen libraries in the north and northwest suburbs merged their computer systems in 1982 to provide far more information to their patrons far more quickly. They were able to call up on a computer screen a list of locations for a particular book and find out where it was on the shelf.

Roosevelt University, or at least its branch two blocks east of the Arlington library building, was hooked up to the Ohio-based Online Computer Library Center that August. That meant anyone at the computer in what was the old North School could locate a book anywhere in the country. Arlington patrons could already locate a book almost anywhere through the North Suburban Library System. But using the OCLC system was just down the line for them.

It looked like the problem of getting information to people was almost solved. The problem of keeping information from people continued to fret certain residents. There are always some people who find certain books unsuitable for public libraries, especially when they are paid for by public funds.

Lois Davidheiser, who didn't necessarily approve of every book on the shelves herself, always counseled potential library board members that they would not be able to vote for their taste but must always keep in mind the good of the public. Frisbie suggested that a library that purchased a book every five minutes, even if the selection was made by thirteen qualified professionals, could not be completely overseen. It was his opinion, even so, that the library professionals made more careful selection than bookstore owners.

It was mostly parents who came to the board, chary of the explicitness of modern fiction and children's way of ranging through the collection without supervision. One citizen objected to tax money going for *Playboy* and *Playgirl.* A young mother browsing with her fourth grader in the children's section found books on homosexuality far too detailed. "Those books should be in the adult section," she advised the staff.

Actually, Frank Dempsey explained, "we allow children to check out adult books" unless parents have their youngsters' library cards punched to prohibit such action.

In the case of *Playboy* Richard Frisbie said that a magazine read by twenty-eight percent of all men who graduated from college represents one aspect of popular American culture. He went on to say that the library board could not debate every title in a library.

Attorney Marlin Smith cited an opinion of the courts that libraries must not censor their collections because some patrons find them objectionable. Jan Tucker reminded the complainants that the board, with a responsibility to the community as a whole, had no right to impose its own morals, tastes, or standards on the patrons. Not that parents didn't have every right to pass on their children's book selections. They just didn't have that right for other parents.

Board members were sympathetic with the residents' concerns. But they could not vote to remove the material. They set up a procedure whereby a committee of librarians, the executive librarian and, finally, the board passed on citizens' complaints. They could take it no farther.

That year they had a million book loans to worry about. And to rejoice in. As Frank Dempsey put it, the increase from 992,496 the year before was not that great, "but there does seem something magical about the one million statistic."

It was magical. It made the circulation of the Arlington Heights Memorial Library the second highest in the state. Only the Chicago library with its eighty-seven branches lent more books to patrons in Illinois in 1981. The community services department circulation had gone up sixty percent; the video cassette circulation, eighty-two percent. A library card in Arlington Heights now entitled a patron to access to over 350,000 volumes and over 50,000 audio-visual items. Besides all those local hands-on possibilities, the library offered patrons computerized access to reference data banks over the country. The library was adding 26,000 items a year. Access to the library via a home television set was at the wire, but not yet a breakthrough.

Continued purchases, augmented services, put the library in the expansion mode once again. When the addition was opened in 1978, there had been unassigned space. For a nominal rent the library had welcomed a social service agency into the space until it should be needed. Northwest Community Services, Inc., provided services for the handicapped and disadvantaged, senior citizens and youth. The money the agency saved on rent by using library space could be spent on programs for their clients.

As part of their common service of the community, the library employed ten young men for ten weeks during the summer of 1982 from the NCS Summer Employment Program. The library also stocked multiple copies of record and cassette courses teaching English to Spanish-speaking persons. By December, 1982, the library board was already talking to Robert Chaney about preliminary estimates and sketches for a move into the unassigned quarters. Audio-visual needed more space. Periodicals were expanding out of their area.

The library was moving into bigger quarters and losing board members Lois Davidheiser, who had been president now for two terms, and Virginia Kucera whose responsibilities as director of admission at Clearbrook Center for the Handicapped was keeping her from expending the energy she'd like on the library board.

Davidheiser, who had served as assistant head of circulation before her ten years on the library board, now went full circle. "Give me a couple of weeks," she told Bill Galaway, director of adult services, "and then I'd like to come in as a volunteer."

She had gone in short order from circulation clerk to assistant head. She had served two terms as president of the board. It would be but a few months and Lois Davidheiser, the board member who thought the library "a super place," advanced from volunteer to volunteer coordinator.

24.
Into The Second Century

Jan Tucker was one volunteer whom Lois Davidheiser had no need to coordinate. A graduate of the University of Michigan, Tucker was primed to do community service by her background and her sense that communities flourish when their settlers sustain them with a rugged and intelligent understructure.

Tucker didn't come to her library volunteer status through the accustomed channels. She was elected to the board of directors. She saw herself as a volunteer nevertheless, and empathized with their perceptions of their role. "I was affronted," Tucker told volunteers at a 1986 luncheon, "when

**Library board president
Jan Tucker**

229

it was said early on that the library couldn't use volunteers because volunteers would not show up.

"I am a volunteer and I come," she told the volunteer honorees. "And I knew you would come. And you did and I did."

Tucker first thought of "volunteering" to run for the board when she read in the *Arlington Heights Herald* that Florence Hendrickson was resigning. As cultural (which she defined as "quality of life") chairperson of the local unit of the American Association of University Women, Tucker was already a library aficianado. "The library *is* this town," Tucker says. "When people come to see the town, I take them to the library."

At that point Tucker knew so little about the library's organization that she asked Hendrickson if she needed a degree in library science to run for the board. Delighted that such an obviously qualified young woman was showing an interest in her beloved library, Hendrickson advised Tucker that the qualification most needed was a willingness to work hard, not an advanced degree. "This isn't going to be an easy job," she told Tucker. "People are going to be looking at you because you are a member of the library board."

Tucker had every intention of working hard. Ready with an agenda for the library, she knew from her experience on other civic boards that effecting her plans would mean diligent study and steady pressure.

Tucker's first priority was to revive the Friends of the Library as allies in the library's task of radiating into the community. Frank Dempsey enthusiastically endorsed this initiative, having learned first-hand the value of Friends. Grace Bowen, a Friends president in the eighties, recalls Tucker as the library board chairperson of public relations who wrote personal letters to former FOL members and Arlington residents in order to muster the reconstructed Friends of the Library. Tucker kept close touch with this group, which had grown to 827 members by Bowen's day, as liaison member from the library board.

Not only was Tucker determined to revitalize the Friends. She was equally bent on gathering a cadre of residents with the leisure to volunteer at the library, people like new resident Phyllis Parlee who found volunteering "a way of putting roots down faster" in a new community.

Not everyone at the library shared Jan Tucker's passion for volunteers "cluttering up the library." The staff had "some fears about volunteers here," Tucker admits, just as other library staffs have had across the country. "They were afraid, at first, that volunteers would take away staff jobs. That hasn't happened. No one has lost a job."

The staff's second misgiving centered around the uncertainty of the volunteers' dependability. Would the volunteers arrive regularly and do the work assigned? It was true that certain potential volunteers announced that they were interested in "meaningful assignments," not Mickey Mouse jobs. These offers were soon weeded out from the steady, willing, talented crew whom volunteer coordinator Pat Scudder found in a round of senior centers, homeowners' associations, and service clubs. Between August, 1979, and September, 1980, Scudder rallied thirty volunteers. Eighteen months later they would have tallied 2,542 hours of service and saved the library $8,827.

To Tucker, reviving the Friends of the Library and establishing the volunteer program were part of the library board's "visionary role. That's part of our responsibility," Tucker says. "We see the forest. The staff sees the trees. That's what we should both be doing."

With the building doubled in size and a capable administrator in place, the library board could step back for some perspective on the intramural practices which they hadn't noticed while they concentrated on picking contractors and choosing furniture. In tandem with the Arlington Heights village board, the library board contracted for two studies by management consultants to discover what better ways the board could serve the staff and the patrons. Changes that came out of the first study, according to Tucker, ranged from the "infinitesimal to the truly important." Two new departments were carved out of the administrative pie: circulation and administrative services.

Like the board, executive librarian Frank Dempsey was now going to have more time for blueprinting future strategies if he could leave personnel, finance, purchasing, maintenance, security, shipping, and receiving activities to new department head Joe Lyon.

Dempsey would be freed to use his masterful skills as "a people person," as Lois Davidheiser characterized his ability—and willingness—to get involved with professional organizations, with the village, with the Chamber of Commerce. You know how much those contacts mean, Davidheiser suggests, "when you need to go to the bank for a computer loan, when you need to pass a referendum, when you need the cooperation of the village."

Jan Tucker admits that the challenge of evaluating and planning "is not nearly so exciting as building a building, but it must be attended to with all deliberate speed."

Tucker's experience as president of the library board has taught her to rely on the board of directors. Every two years during her tenure on the board, she says, the board has been somewhat reconstituted in line with the most recent election. "In all that time, all those people, only two members did not totally pull their weight." Tucker found that no board members were there to be destructive. She was aware that there were candidates who spoke—at least during the campaign—as if they might be destructive forces on the board. "But they were not elected. Those elected by the people came to do good, to help the library be as good as it is, and to better itself. They are a group that genuinely cares about the library."

It is from the people of Arlington Heights that the mandate for a great library comes to the board. As Davdheiser says, "the credit (for the library's excellence) goes to the people of Arlington Heights. They are obviously well-educated and at an interest level that makes them appreciate the library."

Dempsey adds, "The library is good because it is so popular and it is popular because it is so good. Success breeds success." Patrons know when they come to the library that the collection is there to serve them. "The board is not afraid to spend money," according to Dempsey. As a result, a recent survey showed that of the patrons who came into the library for a specific book, sixty-six percent found it. Of those who came in for a book by a certain author or on a certain subject, perhaps a novel by Faulkner or information on the French Revolution, seventy-six percent were satisfied. Of those who came in to browse for something they'd like to read, a "whopping ninety-five percent went home content," according to Dempsey.

In addition, the library has tried to stay at the cutting edge of technology, buying the video cassettes, compact discs, microcomputers, and other audio-visual aids the patrons look for.

A clientele in the habit of thinking of the library when they have informational needs, a board with "intelligence and foresight," a staff that has held fast its hospitable character even as it has increased its competence and efficiency, an executive director with a national reputation, have created the Arlington Heights Memorial Library.

The issue of reciprocal borrowing continues to come up at election time. "I think this will always be a sore point," a board member says, "until we can make people understand how much we derive from our association with the North Suburban Library system, the advantages for our patrons in reciprocal borrowing." A little of the "love/hate" relationship between the Arlington library and NSLS lingers, "because we are so big, I think," a board member suggests.

There is the perennial heating problem. When the library switches from heat to air-conditioning in the spring and air-conditioning to heat in the fall, there are days when the library is uncomfortable.

Basically, however, there is truth in the patron's aphorism that "the library is the one institution in town that can do no wrong." Patrons with that attitude support the library. "I have always felt," board president Jan Tucker says, "that the people of Arlington Heights support their library. If we go to the people and say why we need a new library and this is how we will build it," they'll vote for the library.

In spite of the fact that the Arlington Heights Memorial Library on Dunton was built in 1968 for a population of 68,000 (which is approximately the present population), and that the addition in 1978 doubled the size of the library, the library board may again ask the public for that support Tucker relies on, for a second addition. Once again the library board looks at the prospect of "books on the floor."

That seems almost impossible. The library is already so large. But so is the circulation. Arlington Heights readers took more books out of the library per capita in 1984-85 than residents in any other town of 50,000 and over in the state. An amazing 17.73 books per resident per year.

In 1986 the library board went once again to the village for

234

a gift of land. The town's people population hadn't gone up. But the library's book population was soaring. The library board could see that in two or three years there would not be room on the shelves for the books their patrons wanted.

When executive librarian Frank Dempsey and board president Jan Tucker asked the village board for the last half-block of property between the library building and St. James Street, Tucker produced the newspaper clipping indicating that at the time of the first addition Frank Palmatier had suggested that the remaining parcel be held in abeyance for the library in case of need.

Frank Palmatier, still a member of the finance committee, had not changed his mind. After a recommendation from the finance committee, the village board unanimously agreed that the last half-block should go to the library. The village board's one caveat was that the land be retained for parking so long as the village needed it, for as long as eighteen to twenty-three months.

The library people, well aware how long a plan takes to materialize, gladly complied.

Board president Jan Tucker conjectures that if there is an expansion in the 1980s it will be the "library's last *boom,* the last time we build." Perhaps. But then who could have told the Paul Patrick library board that their library would be vacated in 1968? Or the Florence Hendrickson board that their building would be doubled in 1978?

The Arlington Heights Memorial Library is a library of surprises, as well as a source of gratification, and even elation, to the people of Arlington Heights. Perhaps it should "surprise us by a fine excess," as Keats told us poetry should do. Perhaps it does.

Appendix

HEAD LIBRARIANS THROUGH 1986

Woman's Club Public Library in Shepard Home

1894 - 1909	Lucy and Effie Shepard

Woman's Club Public Library in school

1909 - 1927	Library committee: Mrs. Elizabeth Sigwalt (chair), Mrs. Nellie Noyes Best, Mrs. Eleanor C. Haynes, Mrs. Fred Lorenzen, Miss Edith Jenkinson, Mrs. Mary Dyas, Miss Ella Taylor

Arlington Heights Community Library

1926 - 1927	Mrs. Frances Jenkinson

Arlington Heights Public Library

1927	Mrs. Frances Jenkinson
1928 - 1930	Mrs. Velda Utterback
1930 - 1949	Mrs. Mary Jane Baxter
1949 - 1951	Mrs. Ione Lawbaugh
1951 - 1952	Mrs. Dorothy Mitchell

Arlington Heights Memorial Library

1952 - 1957	Mrs. Florence Kule
1957 - 1962	Mrs. Evelyn Stadelman
1962 - 1969	Mrs. Mary Lee Ewalt
1969 - 1972	Harold J. Ard
1973 -	Frank J. Dempsey

LIBRARY BOARD MEMBERS 1926—1986

Blanche E. Ashton, 1934-1961
Nathaniel Moore Banta, 1926-1932
George C. Beacham, 1966-1970
John Yocum Beaty, 1926-1931
Robert R. Blackburn, 1957-1969
Janet Bowes, 1975-1986
Dorothy Bowlin, 1937-1941
Milton C. Burkhart, 1949-1957
Alfred F. Capps, 1935-1945
George Casey, 1979-1981
Mary Jo Cullen, 1983-
Lois Davidheiser, 1973-1983
Clarence I. Davis, 1932-1941
Robert D. Dibble, 1947-1962
Lawrence Dickerson, 1971-1977
Thomas Dooley, 1973-1981
Charles V. Edward, 1967-1973
William B. Forrest, 1946-1947
Henry R. Franke, 1935-1937
Richard P. Frisbie, 1967-
Helen Graham, 1941-1957
Irma Grose, 1939-1957
Adella Guild, 1926-1934
William Harrah, 1937
John Hathaway, 1981-
Florence Hendrickson, 1957-1975
Francis J. Higgins, 1969-1970
Elsie Murray Hubbard, 1957-1966
Bruce Jarvis, 1931-1935
G. Victor Johnson, 1982-
Philip Jones, 1973
Virginia Z. Kucera, 1977-1983

Roland G. Ley, 1970-1979
Arthur M. McElhose, 1926-1937
Robert L. Melroy, 1970-1975
C. H. Mills, 1945-1949
Charles H. Oestmann, 1962-1967
Paul E. Patrick, 1946-1964
Harold S. Ratliff, 1939-1945
Lillian Russell, 1926-1937
Constance Ryjewski, 1986-
Frank S. Sachs, 1926-1935
Robert J. Scanlan, 1970-1971
Norval Stephens, 1966-1967
Jan Tucker, 1975-
David Unumb, 1983-
Willard F. Vanderbeek, 1941-1947
Nathalie Wallace, 1961-1973
James E. Wood, 1964-1966

Index